OBSERVATIONS OF AN OREO
The Looking-Glass Self

Written by: Vincent D. Carroll
© 2015

(Book Cover art by: Fred Brusseau, Graphic Artist.)

PREFACE

It's been put forth by several great scientists that doing science is just as much a social event as it is anything else. That also goes for graduate students who conduct research writing projects. In their particular case, such students meet regularly with their advisors who in turn evaluate the graduate student's progress at regular intervals and provide instruction on how best to proceed leading toward completion.

I wish I knew individuals who are considered experts in their field of study to consult with in the writing of this publication. I would have enjoyed talking over many of the complex issues surrounding the subject matter this publication considers. At best, I can only consult the books and articles such experts have themselves published. I think of some of the books, written by individuals whose work I admire. Over the years I have pored over their contributions as I longed to better understand human behavior and also too, to obtain a better understanding of black Americans as a group, amid a society that is both progressive and highly diverse in its makeup.

I have to admit to a great deal of envy whenever I would read the preface to their great contributions to human understanding. Because in the writing of such works, the authors who are themselves experts also enlist a legion of other highly credentialed and bright individuals to assist them with advice and critiques of their work. The authors say as much in the preface to their books. The end result of this exchange produces a piece of work that is far better than had it been a solitary process.

Unfortunately this publication was a solitary process. As such, I have been as painstaking in the writing of it as well as how some of the rather sensitive subject matter is approached, as I can be. One of my most ardent goals should I prevail here: I hope to go on to become one of those highly credentialed experts so that I may consult with them in future contributions.

CONTENTS

INTRODUCTION

An Oreo is a cookie made by an American cookie company named Nabisco. That's short for the National Biscuit Company. In the world of snack foods their cookies are well known. Among the varieties they produce there is one in particular that has been co-opted and used as a metaphor to describe a particular kind of African American. This subset of African Americans comprises individuals whose heritage intersects one of the darkest periods in American history known throughout the Western world as the African slave trade.

Nonetheless what distinguish us from all others of this population are some personality traits, our outlook on life in America and a social identity that gives the impression of someone whose way of life is free of the social past of that dark beginning. In short, the grasp we have on life is much more in keeping with that of mainstream society. In fact in some ways, for many of us there is no such thing as "Black America;" only America that is home to people from all over the world.

Throughout the history of the United States there has only been one population of people whose cultural and social identity has been the embodiment of what it means to be American: white Americans. The perception most have of the Oreo is that he or she explicitly attempts to approximate that American archetype. Thus for this subset of African Americans, they are said to be black on the outside and white on the inside, like the cookie.

A quick review of the psychosocial metaphor "Oreo" online turned up several interpretations. The general idea is relatively constant across all instances but like the cookie people's renditions of the concept can be a bit flavorful. The open honesty of a couple of kids saw it this way. "What black kids at my school are if they aren't intolerant and disrespectful trolls who hold up the hallway everyday in between class pushing pot and cutting the entire lunch line. My friend [D]yson from geometry is called an Oreo because he doesn't sell, talks to white people, respects other people and thinks about the future" (www.urbandictionary.com).

Here is the other example. This time from a kid who is African American, yet sees himself as an Oreo. He writes, "I'm black. Even though I live in the projects, I maintain an A average, and speak properly. I have a few white friends, I don't really like watermelon or acting like an animal, and I prefer Gwen Stefani over Crime Mob. Apparently, this makes me an 'Oreo' among my people."

He continues, "Our leaders suffered such great trials so we could get ahead in life. But even hundreds of years later, with the NAACP, the United

Negro College Fund, the equal-opportunity employment act, and the affirmative action policy available to us, we still haven't made any progress. Successful black people are called 'Oreos'" (www.urbandictionary.com).

To see oneself as a process of social interaction is to experience what Charles Horton Cooley (1983) called the "Looking-Glass Self." As we just saw in the examples above, it encompasses the dynamics of how one sees oneself and how one is perceived by others in the social environment. In addition, over the last several decades, research in psychosomatic medicine has discovered that our social realities have a significant impact on our health, quality of life, and even the life span itself (Marmot, M. 2004). Think of it, merely by the way we see our self in society, the inferences we draw from how we think of ourselves and how we think others perceived us (our social standing) has a biological impact. In this vein Cooley wrote "...so in imagination we perceive in another's mind some thought of our appearance, manners, aims, deeds, character, friends, and so on, and are variously affected by it."

So for us Oreos, not unlike all individuals who set about to present themselves in everyday life and manage the impressions others have of us (Goffman, E. 1959), the notion of a self-idea of this sort seems to have three principles elements: the imagination of our appearance to the other person; the imagination of his judgment of that appearance; and some sort of self-feeling, such as pride or mortification." (Taken from: *The Production of Reality* 4th edition, Jodi O'Brien 2006).

Let's take a minute to comprehend the nature of the kind of judgments that are leveled at individuals who are classified as Oreos. To begin with, as we gleaned from the kids who offered us their perception of what an Oreo is, in a general sense, the harsh judgments are not coming from mainstream America. To their way of thinking and to most others, apart from one's heritage, it only makes sense that someone would be so inclined to want to successfully navigate the social environment in which they find themselves. In a basic economic sense it comes down to arriving at a successful way of providing for one's material needs better known as self-preservation. The converse of the motivation accordingly can be understood from several different perspectives; but what perplexes most onlookers can be put to metaphor: "why get in the car and head off in the direction of a place you don't want to go" (Klaus, M. 1995)? And apparently some African Americans aka the Oreo can also understand that reasoning as well.

Sadly however, that leaves a great many in the black community who to this day, see such behavior as attempting to be something one is not. Perhaps one of the most applicable concepts which covers this kind of in-group divisiveness and social coercion is captured in the French phrase "mauvaise foi." Translated into English it means "bad faith." Back in the day, French existentialists used it to convey the philosophical notion that "describes the phenomenon where a human being under pressure from societal forces adopts false values and disowns his/her innate freedom to act authentically" (Wikipedia, 2014). As Black America sees it, or at least those who make such judgments, this would certainly explain the motives of us Oreos and the ostensibly treasonous act of abandoning one own roots for a sense of self—he or she can only "act" the part; hence "acting white."

There is just one snag in this argument. The logic other in-group members use to condemn the Oreo with is one absent of critical thinking. Because to make that claim is to argue indirectly that there is something "essential" about being black which sets the group, in its entirety, far apart from all others racial populations. Racial essentialism is a pre-Darwinian notion that infused Western politics and society that long outlived Darwin himself and in ways has made its way into how most African Americans understand themselves as well. The irony is, racial essentialism is something that has been widely resisted by both black and white populations throughout recent history. And here is the reason why. The idea that blacks are "essentially" different in some important ways, that they are less human, has served as the basis to justify their subjugation and social oppression.

Much of this resistance, the righting of historical wrongs, or social justice, has a substantial history. The centerpiece of this effort is encapsulated in what is known as "the white man's burden." A notion with its own history and mutations as time has gone by. A notion that began as an emblematic piece of Eurocentric racism; but as time has gone by, and the extension of ethical considerations to those who were once understood as inferior metamorphosed into a sincere effort to help the less fortunate around the world. Here in America many other writers have written much about the ways in which the African American community can be helped by mainstream society. To my surprise in the year 2014 some even advocate for reparations. Moreover, many writers of all stripes have written about the help that has already been given to African Americans over the last five decades only to see this group of people fall into greater disarray at a time when personal freedom has never been greater. That was a point of observation made by our young friend who through the social realities of the looking glass self, saw himself as an Oreo because those of his racial population, as well all others, saw him as such.

The consequences of how the majority of American blacks see themselves in society produce real-world results that are readily seen all around us. The remedies to this kind of social orientation are complex and often times it takes something positively transformative and self-determining—even luck—to become aware of one's actual life chances in a modern society such or ours where the march of science and technology propels us continually forward.

Socially these are very paradoxical times: as a nation we have never enjoyed a more eclectic, diverse society. Within the last decade we have twice elected an African-American President and an Attorney General who is black as well. Yet in other very important ways I can't recall a time in recent history wherein Blacks as a group have been more singled out; singled out in ways that does not enhance one's sense of self-worth, social trust and prosocial behaviors. In all of this one thing is for sure, whatever remedies there may be for this state of affairs, there will be nothing magical about the solutions. In other words, this situation will not fix itself. It will require a great deal of critical thinking and action both on the part of society as a whole and Black Americans as individuals.

As I am set to go to publication with this piece I have been made painfully aware of current events regarding a number of high profile shootings of black youths by law enforcement and others as well as the perceptions that linger on in their aftermath. For some it is easy to point to this and say that that is really the true barometer of race relations in America.

I reply by saying that police culture is not indicative of contemporary American culture at large. Speaking in general any agent of "the people" can fall short of the trust we place in them. It can happen with an agent as prestigious as a United States President (i.e. Nixon), it has happened with agencies as sophisticated and complex as the NSA, and surely the potential is there in law enforcement officials to allow base emotions to cloud sound judgment while possessing the ability to exercise deadly force on the spot with practically no real jeopardy attached to such extreme behavior. All of those agencies and agents are examples of the power of social structures and how situations place people in positions of authority and how they are subsequently transformed; doing things perhaps they otherwise would not do outside those roles and contexts (Zimbardo, P.E. 1972).

More specifically it's been observed that people with more contact with a minority group such as social workers, school teachers, and police may have a more pessimistic view of that group's negative traits. They may be able to generalize some unflattering stereotypes to that group that may indeed be statistically accurate (Pinker, S 1997). Therefore to most students of psychology it's absurd to say that one is not swayed by the cumulative effects of such exposure and that it is not a factor in the day to day interactions with those group members. There is ample evidence that social groups that elicit disgust are processed differently by the brain (Harris, L.T. & Fiske, S,T 2007). And as the brain goes, so goes human behavior.

What is more, people, at the same time, possess the ability to step outside that mental schema should they obtain good evidence that an individual member of a generally socially isolated group does not fit the mold of what they had in mind. This thread is a complex one and is deserving of more attention than what I can afford here in this narrative. And yet in many ways it goes to the heart of what this narrative considers.

The point of it all is simply to suggest that to someone who is familiar with those aspects of human nature that are less commendable it just becomes a little easier to think critically about the power of the social situation and to weigh aspects of a complex social situation that may not be popular with everyone.

Also in an ironic twist, those that have raised objections to the notion that social oppression is not the sole cause of the state of affairs in black America, pointing to police brutality, and the high rate of incarceration of black males, have been white persons. This kind of proves my point for me and when we get down to the heart of the matter most responsible citizens regardless of the color of their skin do not want to see the streets of America resemble those of a Middle Eastern country.

Conversely, those with a sense of human nature that is derived from evolutionary theory also understand that nothing is guaranteed about social progress. There is very little about human nature that indemnifies us from reliving past mistakes save our sense of who we are as a people going forward. Specific to the matter at hand, I recall the words of ethics professor Peter Singer (1999), who wrote:

> I have had the great good fortune of having lived most of my life in a multicultural society with a relatively low level of racism; but I know that racist feelings do exist among a significant number of Australians, and they can be stirred up by demagogues. The tragedy of the Balkans has shown only too vividly how ethnic hatred can be revived among people who have lived peacefully with each other for decades. Racism can be learned and unlearned, but racist demagogues hold their torches over flammable material (p.36).

I offer all of that, to say this. It's going to be my assumption that if you're reading a book like this one, by now you've read enough of it already to make a judgment call as to whether a book like this one is for you. Metaphorically speaking, it is all too easy to look at a rash of airplane crashes and assume that that is what happens far more times than not. Do we run a risk by deciding to fly? Yes. But the calculation of that risk is made far easier by knowing about the countless and uneventful takeoffs and successful landings of passenger jets the world over. My assumption then is that those who have decided to carry on have it within themselves to think critically about a topic like this one with its many hot buttons and at times unwieldy complexity. It just about goes without saying that my treatment of this subject matter probably won't be perfect at every turn; yet the subject matter itself is far too important to let that stop me. I steadfastly maintain that this is both a necessary and worthwhile first step toward grappling with issues that are in critical need of understanding better.

******

THE NEWNESS OF AN OLD PERSPECTIVE

Fear of sanctions can coerce behavior whether or not the fear is justified, and whether the sanctions are consensual, conspiratorial, or dictated. Common expectations can lead to concerted behavior.

Tomas C. Schelling

From time to time there have been celebrities and black scholars that have been vocal about black culture and its debilitating effects upon its adherents. And true to form, the kind of criticism that has come their way as a result has been that of a "race traitor" or "uncle tom" and other such things.

But now a new phenomenon is underway within black America, something never seen before among this group. It is called "the school to prison pipeline." In other words children, "preschoolers" of color, are experiencing actual police arrest in the one place no one would have imagined just a decade ago: "in school." Now candidly either one of two things is taking place. Either our society has become more racist over the last decade or there is something endemic to the culture that is playing an important role in this outcome. There is cause and there is effect. And so the real question is: when is enough, enough? Or can anything truly be done about it? Is it simply destiny unfolding? More pointedly, where is the greater betrayal? Does it reside in the Oreo or should black America begin to own some of what is befalling it?

Someone far more brilliant than I will ever live to be once said this:

> There is a sense in which almost no perspective can ever be entirely new. Someone has usually said something similar decades or even centuries earlier. Therefore, when we speak of a perspective being new, it may only be that the world is ready for the first time to take seriously the ideas it embodies, and perhaps also that the ideas have been repackaged in a way that makes them more plausible and accessible to more people (Wallerstein, I. 2004).

There is much about this cultural outlook that is in dire need of review due to the fact that it has ensnared so many in contemporary American society. And "the school to prison pipeline" phenomenon is simply indicative of its ruthlessness. It is up to people to examine better and worse ways of getting things done. And it is that collective attitude that then becomes their culture. A culture that must consistently be burdened with the responsibility of responding to changes both among its group members as well as taking heed to navigating changes in a complex, global society such as the United States.

To be sure, there are meaningful differences between individuals and among racial populations. How those differences are arrived at and how they are understood is the thing that is in great need of a fuller understanding. To criticize those individuals that are labeled as Oreos due to the fact that their behavior portrays an outlook on life that departs from that of a victim of history is to say that all African Americans form an undifferentiated mass of people and that all therefore must fall victim to that collective history. In other words human historical trajectories come encumbered with consequences that can be readily observed today. That's the crux of their argument and moreover that is true. In the case of the Oreo, we seem to be simply more aware of the fact that that history can be a social prison.

The troubling part of it all is that in the very argument they are touting, important or meaningful human differences across populations are brought to the fore by society at large ("white Americans"), racially charged accusations begin to fly, and blame is the result as the black community cleave to their role as history's victims.

For example, here in the state of Washington I recall back in 2010 when a school board member emailed another about racial differences that sparked controversy. Contained within that email was an acknowledgement of racial differences and what he thought was needed to overcome the differences in school achievement in light of the evidence. On the news that evening there was the obligatory rebuttal from a representative of the school board reassuring all that there are no important differences across racial populations. The piece went on to inform the viewer that the school board member in question had been reprimanded for his comments.

Our world presently contains a world of knowledge, a wealth of understanding which can be used to support or refute matter of fact arguments such as essentialism. And for the longest time, Darwinian arguments have been used to support the idea that human hierarchy and the result of racial collisions across history is the natural and rightful order of things. Yet it's Charles Darwin (1859) whom we have to thank for disproving the notion of essentialism among human populations. "[For] Darwin, the intellectual challenge was to demonstrate fundamental similarities between races and therefore, common origins" (Shields & Bhatia 2009).

This is just one of a variety of ways in which this population has really done itself a disservice. Most importantly this disservice is exacting a huge toll on its many members. Such people are ensnared by the very logic that is meant to castigate those of us who have found a way to liberate ourselves from sharing in a self-defeating common fate of all those who have chosen to disengage from society at large. It is one thing to come up with these easily applied metaphors; it's another to think critically about the consequences.

****

THE CENTRAL OBSERVATION

The controlling intelligence understands its own nature, and what it does, and whereon it works.

Marcus Aurelius

The initial interest in writing this piece came as a result of my exposure to consistently debilitating patterns of behavior for African Americans amid a sea change in individual freedom for all members of our modern society. I was struck by the intergenerational fidelity such behaviors retained, and their immediate and obvious ability to undermine individual effort in completing important life tasks in light of the fact that such tasks bear significantly upon quality of life seeking.

Candidly, I contemplated why there appeared to be no substantial reshuffling of priorities and why age-old practices and orientations were rarely called into question, or put upon *"to compete for better and worse ways of getting things done"* (Sowell, T. 1999). Furthermore, on those occasions where such a spirit of renewal was poised to reorder orientations and social outlooks, such inspiration was only able to conjure glimmers of what was envisioned initially. *"Must the poor, always engage in poor behaviors?"* (Lynch et al. 1997).

In generations past, the assignment of blame for such outcomes always had the populace at large to hold accountable for the preponderance of the explanatory calculus regarding these invidious social outcomes. However, as this atavistic explanation for the ongoing status quo continues its march towards becoming a relic—and conversely, as "the tangle of pathologies" (Moynihan, Daniel 1965); (Hymowitz, K 2005) among African Americans across vital indexes both endures and in some cases increases in intensity—a much needed paradigm shift in how we go about understanding this dilemma and providing narratives has become imperative.

Identity is a complex phenomenon. It's multifaceted and depending upon the power of the social situation, it can be highly dynamic. For instance as Americans we all share a national identity. From there one's personal identity will also include biases as to race, a particular state in the union, political affiliations, sporting teams, etc.

All of these domains and the way in which we identify with them also have the potential to cause us to act in ways which can spark intense competition among out-group members, or benevolence leading to cooperation for ingroup members.

The same can absolutely be said about diverse human populations across history. What's more, this aspect of our sense of self (race: one's sense of peoplehood) exerts a powerful influence over how we see the world, and our place in it. It's functional in that it seems to answer the question of why we need a social past. And whether we want it to or not, it anchors everything we know about ourselves.

Our social/historical past shapes our sense of self and our group identity or peoplehood. From it we get our cultural identity—about which both ingroup members and out-group members as well as the individual in question tend to hold himself accountable to; or if need be find strong reason why he or she shouldn't. Either way one's social past plays a central role in this consideration.

Yet little known, mangled and mislabeled by the torrents of human history is another significant contributor to how we know ourselves. As human beings, we all possess a biological self. This is important because all things psychological, social and cultural are simultaneously biological (Myers, D.G. 2004) (Richerson, Boyd, Henrich 2010). In today's world understanding human psychology means staying abreast of how the integration of all of the features of the human person contribute to produce human behavior (Sokol & Stroud 2007). "The abyss between biological and social levels of organization is a human construction, however, one that must be bridged to achieve a complete understanding of human behavior" (Cacioppo, J.T. 2000) (Cacioppo et al. 2002).

At the forefront in such an endeavor is evolutionary theory. The tenets of evolution by natural selection unequivocally conclude that biological life on planet earth varies as a matter of course (Darwin, C. 1859). Understanding the impact of evolution on the human person as to how and why humans vary is to understand its role in the survival of humankind from eons ago to present day (Buss, D.M. 1999), (Rowe, D.C. 2005), (Balaresque, P.L. et al. 2007),(Gillian, R.B. et al. 2011).

Moreover, as clear-cut advances are made in human genomics, neuroscience, and biotechnology; our understanding of the human person should also increase with such knowledge given the fact that in doing so, such knowledge has already begun to prove its worth by allowing professionals to better understand and treat everything from mental illnesses to how social standing and self-worth can adversely impact human health and wellbeing (Marmot, M. 2004). Thus, the integration of an array of disciplines is demonstrating conclusively that not only do humans vary, but in a diverse society such as ours, human variation is far better understood than ignored (Risch, N. et al. 2007).

Also, in a departure from the ways in which such a discussion have gone in the past. Human history can no longer be sidestepped in favor of a hard target search of human biology exclusively. As Jared Diamond (1999) suspected some 15 years ago, human history has become a vital piece in explaining the science of biological realities. Importantly, it is from a proper perspective on history that we come to understand the role of "the construction of social realities" and the impact it had and has; both in perpetuating intergenerational social stations and human variation (Symons, D. 1992).

In the age of human genomics, we become aware of novel changes in genes, and gene frequencies giving way to human diversity. Bona fide explanations of human variation or individual differences cannot move forward devoid of human history, devoid of both the physical, cultural and social environments out of which emerged human diversity (Richerson, P.J. et al. 2010).

Accordingly, to understand human behavior at any depth, one must understand humanity's evolutionary past. That past includes the environment which brought about anatomically modern humans (*h. sapiens*). That past includes, the disparate regional environments out of which come populational differences across race and cultures. And especially, that past includes the run-away social and cultural competitions among the world's peoples in vying for control of the earth's resources and its people.

Most integral to this reality are the autocatalytic processes differential culture and genes engage cooperatively, to better *adapt*—the individual at one level, and human groups in significant ways at another—to the fallout of those competitions.

Further on downstream, all of this means that we must critically consider the ramifying effects of human hierarchy which follows naturally from the consequences of those fated human competitions across the last ten thousand years of human history. A time period which is at the origin of much of the significant human diversity we observe today.

And the reasons why are clear; that human activity continues to carry a high historical mortgage which at present is perpetuating a recurrent social cosmology among the world's populations. This phenomenon can be easily observed in a nation of diverse human populations such as ours. The observation doesn't dissipate when we look comparatively across the globe.

Due to the fact that I myself possess a group identity (African American) which currently is at maximum risk in America's contemporary society because of all that has been mentioned, this essay is a snapshot of a much larger contribution I hope to make in advancing human understanding, about what it means to be human.   The hope then, is that where such information was used in the past to erect walls among the world's racial populations, and therewith provide a plausible rationale for denying some their humanity, perhaps in these contemporary times, we can take the same subject matter, due to its staying power and relevance, and reexamine it through the lens of the revolutionary advances in human genomics and neuroscience of the modern era. And once aptly reconnoitered, we can begin to build bridges to the best humanity has to offer by simply providing information that is only meant to broaden our understanding of what it means to be human. This is the first in a series that is meant to unpack all that is written above.

****

THE NEED TO BELONG

Deep in our bones, for example, we are social beings. There is no escaping it. We can't survive on our own when we're young, and it doesn't get a whole lot easier later on. We need to feel that we belong to something bigger than ourselves, whether it's a family, or a team, or a society. We look to other people to tell us that we measure up, that we matter, that we're okay.

Allan G. Johnson 2001

For the longest time, human populations of color have had to live with the ignoble feeling that they were not as human as all other humans around them. The human spirit can be broken, and for sure that had been the case with Africans and African Americans. The effects of this linger on and it is something that can be transmitted across time and generations by way of a population's culture. Today we can better understand the long-run consequences of this as learned helplessness and one of its outcomes can be a culture of poverty. "We *learn* to be human, and our learning depends on and is achieved through interaction with other humans" (O'Brien, J. 2006).

In my search for answers to some of the complex human issues listed in the central observation, it meant that I would have to study material that had long been branded as anathema to the existence of people of color. Such things as evolutionary theory, game theory and human sociality, human behavioral ecology, genetics and its influences upon human behavior and populations. Sometimes the writers of such material may be expert in their field, but have a lousy bedside manner in going about writing about human differences. To my mind, when it's done in this fashion, it can do more harm than good even as it may very well promote our understanding of ourselves and the world around us.

I recall one instance in particular in which I was reduced to nothing. My sense of humanity had all but vanished and the feeling of being hollowed out, existentially eviscerated by what I read is almost indescribable. The book I was reading is entitled "Race: Evolution & Behavior" (1999) by J. Philippe Ruston. On page 29 of the special abridged edition there is this black infant that is being manipulated by a set of white hands and the idea of this was meant to show actual proof by way of a photograph that black infants, as a group, develop physically sooner than infants from other racial populations. The picture itself was taken in 1958 and there is something about the photograph that is indicative of that time period in American history. A time when the farce of "separate but equal" ruled racial interaction, a time that also conveyed the notion: no matter what black

17

Americans did to gain entry into mainstream, the matter of fact answer to their best efforts was that they will never belong.

As for my reading of that book; I read it to completion due to the fact that it does in fact explain something significant about human behavior and populational differences due to human evolution subsequent to human groups leaving Africa and settling in disparate parts of the world. But I understand if I am among a handful of people of color that bothered to read Rushton's book because in the words of Don Henley of the 1970s rock group "The Eagles" it was "hard to come away with anything that feels like dignity... hard to get home with any pride" in doing so. Therefore, one of the things I hope to do over the long haul is to present research of the sort that Rushton presented but without the demoralizing existential hurt that for the longest time, experts and researchers presented, but perhaps without considering that such material could reach individuals of a divergent historical human trajectory.

There is a great deal of research that shows that social isolation kills. If there is one message that I would want to make clear it is that one. And it's a point of departure for many in Black America because it is a natural inclination to want to disengage from social situations and interactions where one feels less confident and socially accepted. Had I done that in connection to that book I read some time ago; in all likelihood I would not have followed my passion to better understand human behavior and also understand myself as an individual with a lineage of human subjugation that seems to stymie so many like myself in today's world. And that's worth knowing about.

In a complex society such as ours, to disengage, to socially isolate oneself is to ensure one's defeat. The pain of exclusion can be formidable; there is no doubting that. But it pales in comparison to what takes place over the course of the life span of those who do not engage. Among many other things, it leads to a thought life fraught with substantial life regret and it's imminently connected with the people we see all around us regardless of their racial makeup simply because we all have a need to belong.

****

BELONGINGNESS: A BASIC HUMAN MOTIVATION

On the other hand man evolved as a social animal, and he can neither develop normally nor long function successfully except in association with other human beings.

Rene Dubos

There isn't a more commonplace mantra in psychology than the one which says that "humans are social creatures." It is because we have a need to belong. The human need to belong is a basic human motivation. Most who are familiar with the history of psychology will recall Abraham Maslow's (1943) "hierarchy of needs"—a set of needs which drives human motivation. Within that "hierarchy" the need to belong surfaces soon after physiological needs such as food, water and shelter has been satisfied. However, that hierarchy is not as linear as he presented it. Often times, in providing for those more fundamental needs, doing so also includes social interaction which in turn satisfies belongingness needs.

Yale's professor of bioethics Peter Singer (2000) in conversing about human attributes that exhibit "little variation across cultures" he too writes that "we are social beings... the fact that human beings, unlike, say, orangutans, generally do not live alone. Our readiness to form cooperative relationships, and to recognize reciprocal obligations, is another human universal."

One of the central themes of this narrative is to argue for the notion of how we are all interconnected, influencing and being influenced by all those around us. It is in that respect that we belong to each other, because all humans belong to the human race and in terms of perspectives, it is in this fashion that I believe it is impossible to tell the story of African Americans without touching upon that of white America. In addition it is impossible to tell the story of America as the United States without including the forced contributions of African slaves and the legacies that such an asymmetrical relationship has spawned.

But it's the year 2015, and at bottom what many in our modern society are in search of is a new way of going forward; by going forward; and not going forward by going back; if that makes any sense. I think the cultural psychologist Hazel Markus said it best: "Carrying history on your back gets outright tiring, especially when that history is very different than what is needed to succeed in socially competitive environments" (Markus, H . 2008). The paradox continues on because in ways, it is only by understanding and appreciating what history has wrought in human populations, and the pitting of individuals from the various human groups against each other in open social competitions in contemporary society, that we can begin to move forward in any authentic sense.

For instance how are we to understand the observation made of the majority of black Americans who continue to fail in spite of all the help that they've been given? In contemplating the real world consequences, one American citizen observed this: "[I]f they feel therefore inferior, that is likely to be bad for social equality... it's bad even if they fail as a result of their own free will—worse, maybe, since then they have nobody to blame" (Klaus, M. 1992).

Ostensibly, for most African Americans the only thing to do in these situations is to fall back upon one's role as history's victims as opposed to allowing the clarity of the current situation to guide the nature of their self-reflection. And it's just that doing the former doesn't get such people anywhere, anymore; especially in socially competitive environments. All around us we see people whose life regret is exhibited on their faces and in their bodies in the form of debilitating health and a life that is in default. And it's inexorably connected to being connected with and to other people. It is socially transactional.

What is more, due to the historical trajectory of African Americans, individual black Americans today experience the need to belong or conversely the existential angst of being socially adrift more intensely than perhaps many other individuals from the various human populations which comprise our society. In a study that examines life regrets and the need to belong researchers have found that a) "the need to belong constitutes one of the most pivotal of human motives. Moreover, faced with social rejection, mental and physical health suffers dramatically" (Cacioppo & Hawkley 2009), (Leary 1990). And b) "Regrets with high social impact [such as the social stigma associated with failure] were more intense than regrets with low impact....for instance, perhaps interpersonal regrets are more intense because of their involvement of other people [which] makes it easier to adopt a looking glass self... and thus a more critical view of oneself" (Morrison, M. et al. 2012). So yes! "It's worse" since such persons "have no one to blame" and the depth of embarrassment as a result of such existential despair carries the potential to rob its victims of all initiative to override this kind of pernicious internalized helplessness.

From the time of Maslow to the present, the study of scientific psychology has advanced. Yet for the longest time in the study of psychology it was taken as a given that a need as basic as a need to belong did not really require any empirical research. The reason being just about all psychological research of one shade or another implicitly assumed the need to belong as an underlying motivation which directed human action.

Curious about the near absence of research in this area, researchers Roy Baumeister and Mark Leary (1995) did a literature review on "the need to belong and the desire for interpersonal attachment as a fundamental human motivation." They found that "even at a quick glance at research on social behavior from the perspective of the belongingness hypothesis raises the possibility that much of what humans do is done in the service of belongingness."

From that literature review the researchers observed these commonalities as a way of evaluating the belongingness hypothesis as being fundamental to human motivation:

- Produce effects readily under all but adverse conditions
- Have affective (emotional) consequences
- Direct cognitive processes
- Lead to ill effects (such as on health or adjustment) when thwarted
- Elicit goal-oriented behaviors designed to satisfy it
- Be universal in the sense of applying to all people
- Not be derivative of other motives
- Affect a broad variety of behaviors
- Have implications which go beyond immediate psychological functioning

Also too due to the great diversity of American society, there is something very important to be said for living in close geographical proximity with individuals from various racial, ethnic, religious, historical, economic and sociological backgrounds. American society has progressed to a point where all individuals are free to move about the nation and pursue their best life hopes unrestrained by social oppression. This increases the ways in which individuals can arrive at the feeling of belongingness. In addition we have social media and networking across the globe which in ways, continues to erode those categorical walls that once maintained various human groups at a greater social and psychological distance from each other in times previous.

Political scientist Francis Fukuyama understands this well. In elaborating on "The Great Disruptions" (1999) of human history he sees the information age having a profound effect upon our freedom of choice. Specifically "a society built around information tends to produce more of the two things people value most in a modern democracy: freedom and equality" (p.4).

I once heard it said that "the mind is a relative making machine." And while "[p]reserving cultural diversity is considered a supreme virtue today... the members of the diverse cultures don't always see it that way. People have wants and needs, and when cultures rub shoulders, people in one culture are bound to notice when their neighbors are satisfying those desires better than they are" (Pinker, S. 2002 p.66).

From the outline on human belongingness we see that important cognitive and emotional factors play a role as we navigate the social environment in search of key interpersonal attachments that fills that need. In other words we tend to put some thought into and assign priority to how to belong given who we think we are and among whom should we seek approval. "Intelligent thought is generally recognized as the most important adaptive trait among human beings, and so it seems reasonable to assume that issues of fundamental concern and importance are likely to be the focus of cognitive activity" (Baumeister & Leary 1995).

In terms of "emotional consequences" to satisfy belongingness needs also means to maintain ways of protecting the self as we seek to satisfy the need to belong. As individuals we tend not to hang out with people who dislike us because as I mentioned earlier the pain of exclusion can shatter our sense of self, says psychologist Kipling D. Williams (2011). The need for approval (positive affect) is therefore pivotal in the formation of interpersonal attachment where one feels like they belong. Because where humans are concerned, be they Oreos; vanilla or chocolate cookies; all persons seek social acceptance and the validation of one's humanity. "These emotions are inherently social: when one feels anger at a lack of recognition, one does not want a material object outside the body; rather, one wants evidence of a mental state—recognition—on the part of another's subjective consciousness" (Fukuyama, F. 1995).

In the literature review of the need to belong the writers illustrated how interpersonal attachments were motivated to some degree by the bullet points listed above. But just like most other human needs, the ways and mannerisms of how individuals go about satisfying them is embedded in their culture. Baumeister and Leary (1995) acknowledge as much. They also recognize that where culture is concerned there will be "individual differences in strength and intensity, as well as cultural and individual variation in how people express and satisfy the need." Where those with a hybrid social identity such as Oreos, the pairing of one's cultural identity and of an individual's sense of self may not always, and under all conditions, be in total agreement.

A good example of this is seen in the observations of Cornel West (1993). He wrote "the choice of becoming a black intellectual is an act of self-imposed marginality in the black community; it assures a peripheral status in and to the black community." Here he offers us a sound example of how goal-directed behaviors intersect the need for approval. Also I would add as another point of departure of this narrative is that where the Oreo is concerned; our social identity is far more complex than the meeting of material and economic needs. In an ironic way it's really like saying that birds of a feather flock together. Where "the feather" is a value proposition which forms the psychological basis for values importance, tradeoffs, and responses to value-laden rhetoric (Bain, P.G. et al. 2006).

Personal satisfaction has just as much to do with personal liberation and the exploration of the self as it does with the meeting of more basic physiological and economic needs. The fulfillment of goal-directed behaviors not only enhances belongingness; it also has a way of defining and/or redefining the nature of one's tribe which can easily transcend race and ethnicity while doing wonders for one's sense of self, self-esteem and sense of agency. On a personal level that has been my experience.

Goal-directed behaviors are the everyday application of "where" and "who" we want to be at some future date. These mental frames we have of ourselves at some future date are called "possible selves" (Markus and Nurius, 1986, 1987). They go hand in hand with achievement and human achievement is something we engage in as a means of satisfying and reaffirming our belongingness needs. "People prefer achievements that are validated, recognized and valued by others over solitary achievements, so there may be a substantial interpersonal component behind the need for achievement" say belongingness researchers Baumeister and Leary (1995). Thus it can said that our concept of our future self now and its possible future fulfillment, underscores motivations for interpersonal attachments, guides our understanding of the social and cultural world around us, and establishes an ongoing personal narrative set to "continuous play" as we seek to actualize that future frame. As we go about this behavior, social signals (both explicit and tacit) from the world around us reveal to us to whom we belong as we align the need to belong with the need for approval from select others as we approve of ourselves in doing so via the looking glass self.

There is such a thing as human variety and so it should not strike us as odd that this phenomenon holds true even among African Americans as a population. Thus to comprehend the Oreo is achieved in the same fashion to which we comprehend all persons in a complex society.

> The life of an individual cannot be adequately understood without reference to the institutions within which his biography is enacted... it may well be that the most radical discovery within recent psychology and social science is the discovery of how so many of the most intimate features of the person are socially patterned and even implanted (*The Sociological Imagination*, C. Wright Mills 1959, p. 161).

****

Thus, all of the relevant research on belongingness seems to bring us to a conclusion which Herman Melville observed some time ago. Indeed, it is a seminal point on human belongingness, and interpersonal attachment as a condition of being human that is inescapable regardless of an individual or population's attempts to do otherwise. He said, *"we cannot live only for ourselves. A thousand fibers connect us with our fellow men; and among those fibers, as sympathetic threads, our actions run as causes, they come back to us as effects."*

To my mind nothing sums up race relations in this nation quite like that keen insight. In considering the literature review of Baumeister & Leary (1995) and the fundamental components which shapes belongingness needs, they said that the need to belong will lead to ill effects when thwarted. To help us understand just how important and complex an issue we have on our hands going forward, evolutionary theorist Richard G. Wilkinson (2000) in his study of "Hierarchies, Health and Human Evolution" amplifies the practicality of Melville's insight. He writes:

> As the evolutionary biologist Richard Alexander has pointed out, the primary hostile force of nature encountered by human beings is other humans. Conflicts of interest are pervasive, and, to paraphrase Alexander, the competitive strivings of other members of our species become the most salient feature of our evolutionary landscape. By virtue of having all the same needs, other members of our own species are our most feared competitors—for housing, jobs, sexual partners, food, clothing, and so on. But they are also our only source of help, friendship, assistance, learning, care and protection. This means that the quality of social relationships has always been vital to our material welfare. Depending on our relations with others, we could gain or lose the world (p.8).

Once again social isolation kills. And if "Black America" as a self-contained, functional, Balkanized entity had a good thing going within the larger context of American society then none of the health, social and psychological issues mentioned by Baumeister and Leary should manifest themselves within the population. Yet where the African American community is concerned nothing could be farther from the truth. To date, this community is riddled with a range of social, health and psychological afflictions.

The act of self-kill or suicide is a key indicator of how healthy a connection an individual or population has with those around them. The rate of suicide among black males led the nation over a period of five years. And the suicide rate has doubled for black males nationally since 1980, making it the third leading cause of death among African American males, ages 15 to 24 according to the C.D.C. (jsonline.com).

24

From the literature review "[t]he relevance of belongingness to suicide was suggested nearly a century ago by Emile Durkheim (1897/1963). His seminal work proposed that suicide could be explained as a result of a failure of social integration. People who are well integrated into society by multiple and strong relationships are unlikely to commit suicide, whereas unintegrated people are more likely to kill themselves" report Baumeister and Leary (1995).

Indeed, there is a wide web of social, intellectual and health disparities that plague the black community. And it is they that must find a way to better engage society at large if they ever hope to rid themselves of the ill-effects of the ongoing social disengagement. The late Maya Angelou sought such remedies and worked to counteract such effects. In a piece done on her by *Huff Post (Black Voices)* in 2012 she is quoted as saying that the disparities that exist among those in the black community "are embarrassing." And she saw self-awareness and participation as a way of escaping preventable illness. In the piece she says that "the biggest gift I can give anybody: *Wake up, be aware of who you are, [and] what you're doing.*" These are words to live by.

But I am more intrigued by what she did not say. She did not place undue blame for something that is personally preventable on the public at large. I guess it's the idea that not everything that hamstrings black progress is someone else's fault. If indeed, mainstream America had a nationwide conspiracy underway, as some seem to suggest, to trample people of color; she of all people would know what that looks like. Maya Angelou was a participant in the civil rights movement of the 1960s and worked closely with Martin Luther King. If you know anything about Maya Angelou's life, you know it was not exactly an easy one. But she lived it, based in the present, going forward into the future, not the past.

By comparison, the intellectual magazine *"The Atlantic"* (June 2014) featured a front-page article that concerned itself with reparations to African Americans for a history of human subjugation. The piece has this header:

> "Two hundred and fifty years of slavery. Ninety years of Jim Crow. Sixty years of separate but equal. Thirty-five years of racist housing policy. Until we reckon with our compounding moral debts, America will never be whole."

Candidly my initial reaction to this article went something like this. "It's amazing...individual African Americans as citizens occupy every socioeconomic level we have. And yes, it's true that the vast majority of Blacks subsist at the lower rungs of the socioeconomic ladder. But the reasons why, as well as the remedy for this extend far beyond talking the

American public into a payday as a way of solving that problem. It's little wonder that individual African Americans have a hard time getting beyond being perceived as an 'undifferentiated mass of people'."

Yes! As the header of that piece states; all of that is true. All of that did happen! But at what point do such people stop using it as a reason to fail... at what point do they stop living in the past... and using it to exploit a historical guilt and shame in the hopes that blame for what is taking place now can all be passed off, in its entirety, to the broader society. As we read in the introduction, a kid who understood himself as an Oreo had the wherewithal to see that a host of sweeping programs geared toward the black community, spanning more than half a century, has had little to no effect.

According to the article in *The Atlantic* just about anything blacks do, wouldn't be sufficient to save themselves. At several points in the article I got the impression that there is a white person lurking behind every tree ready to pounce on any persons of color with the motivation to achieve something worthwhile in their lives. After painting a picture of the abject bleakness with which African Americans are forced to abide in; the language of the article gave the impression that the only social strategy available to blacks is to do nothing except wait on a reparations pay out. Something even the writer of the article says is not forthcoming.

As an individual with an African American ancestry, I'm kind of sick of coming across articles and arguments like this. Mainly because I think they do more harm than good. The deeper we go back into history with a tone and tenor characteristic of the article in *The Atlantic*, the deeper and polarizing is its effect upon people of today. Most Americans do not need this shoved in their face in order to get them to consider ways of helping. People for the most part already have a sense of these things and I can prove it.

I looked up this nation's contributions to Haiti in the aftermath of the devastation of the 2010 earthquake which rocked the island nation. In doing so I thought that such data could be used as a social barometer to indicate whether this nation as a whole, harbors the "trenchant" racism that had been alluded to in that article. What I found was that, it was the United States which led the world in its commitment to help Haiti recover from that natural disaster, by pledging $3.6 billion of the total $10 billion in aid promised by nations around the world. That is the money stream directly from the U.S government. In the days following the earthquake, philanthropy.com on January 27, 2010 reported this:

> Contributions continue to pour in for relief efforts in Haiti. Fifteen days after the massive   earthquake struck, donors have contributed more than

$528 million dollars to 40 U.S. nonprofit groups... the pace of giving for Haiti is running ahead of the amount donated in the same period after the September 11 attacks of 2001 and the Asian tsunamis in 2004, but slower than the   outpouring of gifts after the flooding caused by Hurricane Katrina in 2005. In the eight days   after the flooding started in New Orleans, Americans gave at least $580 million for relief efforts.

These are hard facts, not someone's subjective impressions of the degree of explicit racism they insist is still in existence in contemporary America. And there is more. Right here in Seattle, philanthropist Floyd Jones, a Caucasian, observed legal system biases toward blacks and the poor and donated 10 million dollars to the ACLU, an organization dedicated to social justice for all (*The Seattle Times*, 10/14/2014). "The Innocence Project" an organization dedicated to freeing wrongly accused individuals using DNA testing has as of this date achieved the exoneration of 202 African Americans of the total 321 people freed by its efforts. On the international scene, literally tens of billions of dollars have been poured into helping the individuals of developing nations on the African continent. People and organizations continue to give, withstanding the dismal 50 years of evidence which shows that all that aid has done little good.

Does that mean that everything in America is perfect? No... when dealing with people things rarely are. However, it's a far cry from how that article framed the state of affairs in contemporary American life. Perhaps it's a matter of what one decides to look at in making such determinations. It is this writer's notion that perhaps the time has come where we should be far more careful about discharging these sweeping declarations of blame and creating narratives laced with ad hominem phraseology designed to invoke emotions which are more befitting of a bygone era. Today's issues call for far more contemplation than what the historical defaults have left us with. Blame in today's America seems to terminate in inertia—you can go nowhere with it. Moreover what is sorely needed going forward is to foster and cultivate a greater sense of belongingness even as current events may, sometimes, work in a way that seems to contradict that progress. After all, historically, if any one group has paid the price of admission into mainstream America, it is ours. For us Oreos, we seem to be about acting like it by turning past tragedies into today's triumph.

****

A WORLD OF KNOWLEDGE

I am always doing that which I cannot do, in order that I may learn how to do it.

Pablo Picasso

Sometimes I find it strange that we are awash in a world of information, of knowledge; the ability to know more about the things which really impact our lives and yet so few of us avail ourselves of that world of knowledge. I would think that doing so would be especially true in cases where one's life chances are adversely impacted should they continue on in ignorance of the world around them. After all, out of our evolutionary past, that has been the case. Learning has allowed humankind to modify its behavior in an adaptive way in response to sensory feedback. For eons learning has allowed humans to cross a 'valley' of low fitness in a complex adaptive landscape to one where they reached a higher adaptive peak. Indeed it was the ability to learn that allowed our species to move out of Africa and into every region of the globe, and if need be, to thrive there (Sutter, M. & Kaweck, T.J. 2009).

Be that as it may. I find such ignorance strange now, but I didn't while growing up and for most of my young adult life. In fact, growing up fatherless and fearful of the social environment in which I found myself; at the time it made perfect sense to me that the one place I really didn't need to be was in school. But that's the nature of cultures that are specific to a population of people; it shapes how its adherents see the world. As a struggling family, we were constantly pressed to consider more urgent needs, such as food, keeping the water from being shut off for non-payment, and the same went for the electricity.

In addition, or perhaps more as a consequence of that situation, my ways of escaping psychologically was to day-dream to the point of pathology. By this I mean, I could not stop myself from being taken over in this way. I was avoidant, introverted and painfully shy. All these are traits you really don't want as a child growing up in a challenging environment, if being mentally present is something that is a prerequisite for doing well in school. I could have had Albert Einstein as my teacher and it wouldn't have mattered.

The point I'm attempting to make is that we are not all born equal in terms of talents and abilities, nor do we all have the same nurturing environments which allows for the expression of the talents and abilities we might possess. When considering how to best assist those who may not have the most nurturing social environments, to only consider the social environment to the exclusion of all other aspects of the human person is to enfeeble any attempt at helping them.

For the longest time, many of those who championed such ideas as "no child left behind" and other social justice issues were quick to write off anything which suggested that there were meaningful human differences across populations. And make no mistake, I believe that everything should be done to provide children with the best education possible. Already on the international scene our kids' scholastic achievements lag far behind the bulk of technologically advanced nations and even some developing nations.

But high level, "advance placement" performance is one thing and sufficiently educating a child on the basics is another. When programs such as "no child left behind" fail and continue to fail in spite of everything, it says that we are failing at meeting the bare essentials of education. And specifically, it probably won't come as a surprise that African American kids are the poster child for failure in this arena. A piece done by *U.S. News & World Report* (June 27, 2013) states that our "high school kids have made no progress in 40 years." The writer goes on to offer this:

> "If we have a crisis in American education, it is this: That we aren't yet moving fast enough to educate the 'minorities' who will soon comprise a 'new majority' of our children nearly as well as we educate the old majority," said Kati Haycock, president of The Education Trust, an organization that promotes closing achievement gaps.

> "At best, students of color are just now performing at the level of white students a generation ago," she added in a released statement. And it's important to hint at the size of the disparity she is alluding to by emphasizing "at best."

To personalize this point, I once took a class on life span psychology or developmental psychology, it is also called. Essentially, life span psychology is "the field of study that examines patterns of growth, change, and stability in behavior that occurs throughout the entire life span" (Feldman, F.S. 2003). As you can imagine, this is a really wide field of study. In addition, when we begin to look at the life span in terms of important milestones, or segments which take place in the life of a human; it becomes apparent how important each stage of growth is in providing the nexus from one stage to another. For instance there are "beginnings" and the start of life. This is where the complexities of prenatal, birth and newborn infancy are studied. Then there is "infancy forming" which can be called "the foundations of life." This includes physical, cognitive, social and personality development. And truly it is the foundation because much of who and what we are in life was pretty much decided during this time period.

Then there are all the other important periods of the life span that are stacked, if you will onto that foundation. These include "the preschool years, the middle school years, adolescence, early adulthood, middle adulthood, late adulthood and endings" (Feldman, F.S. 2003).

Due to the fact that we are a diverse society, one of the things the field considers is differences across racial populations. Let me tell you, it is one thing to observe human differences around us which lend themselves to making important distinctions as need be. It is quite another to closely examine and interpret statistics across racial populations and their meanings to the people in question. During this course, much of it began to mimic that of a competitive horse race among populations. And at each turn, black Americans, as a group, were always "bringing up the rear" as they say. As the only black American in the class it was quite something to sit there and see all of that in such a fashion.

And sadly, the old adage, "if current trends continue" doesn't even apply where blacks rate as a group in terms of the total cosmology of social life in our nation because not only will the current trends continue, everything one could look at suggests that it will only grow in intensity.

Today, around the world and here in America we are getting to a place where explanations of what is happening around us and in us are in need of far more than just the incomplete arguments of yesteryear. There is a world of knowledge that is in the midst of transforming how we know and understand ourselves. But to avail ourselves of it, it's going to take a fresh look at some old perspectives. *"The growth of biological thought"* (Mayr Ernst 2000) can also be understood like this, for "(n)o field of science has changed more, or changed the world more, in the last 50 years than genetics—the study of how our physical and behavioral traits are inherited. The field crowning achievement may have been the spelling out of genetic secrets by the human genome project, but scientific and technological advances in genetics have transformed agriculture, biology medicine, zoology, and even fields such as anthropology and forensic science" (Cohen, P 2006/ New Scientist).

Today the more informed among us readily understand that you can't have one (nature) without the other (nurture). And in terms of which is more important, nature or nurture, that's like asking which is more important in creating a table, the length, width or height? Dismiss either of those and we no longer have a fully-fledged table on our hands.

In like manner "The nature of the genetic leash and the role of culture can now be better understood, as follows. Certain cultural norms also survive and reproduce better than competing norms, causing culture to evolve in a track parallel to and usually much faster than genetic evolution"

(E.O. Wilson 1999). This also means that in certain instances a dire situation can arise such as a culture of poverty. Where the staying power of that culture has a way of catabolizing human will power to sustain itself, it undermines hopes, and the best laid plans for change and with each successive generation. It has a way of making its captives more suited to the socio-cultural environment it has established as opposed to some other in which new learning is required to succeed at making adaptive changes on important life tasks. In other words, culture drive human evolution (Henrich, J. 2011).

Much of this can be hard pills to shallow. As commented on by one of the world's foremost evolutionary biologists William D. Hamilton (1936-2000) "geneticists were leery of anything that smacked of eugenics. That included most of all applications to understanding social behavior, something we have always been a little touchy about. If nature was nasty, rude, or bawdy, better not to know about it, let alone the public know" (*Behavioral Ecology*, Vol.12 No. 3: 261-268).

But the clash of biological findings and human values has a long and turbulent relationship. Ernst Mayr (1982) says "as a consequence, democracy can be interpreted to assert not only equality before the law but essentialistic identity in all respects. This is expressed in the claim, 'All men are *created* equal,' which is something very different from the statement 'All men have equal rights to the law and are equal before the law.' Anyone who believes in the genetic uniqueness of every individual thereby believes in the conclusion, 'No two individuals are *created* equal' " (emphasis his, p.79). For a must read on how we as a society should move forward in the light of the fact that all around us we observe evidence which contradicts the more fashionable explanations for it, see Peter Singer's "A Darwinian Left: Politics, Evolution and Cooperation" (1999).

We will need such contributions to replace old and longstanding narratives which were more geared toward promoting and maintaining social harmony—"a noble lie"—than they were at tackling the sometimes harshness of human nature as seen across populations right here in America. Here is an example, "the idea of race so intrinsic a part of American social life is a surprisingly ephemeral one" (Marks, J. 2010) writes one expert. Currently, we are observing that is simply not true.

People have long had a sense that more was needed in the explanation of human behavior even as they acquiesced to the noble lie for the greater good. The history books are filled with public versus private gleanings on human diversity by persons whose scholarship has been used to promote social harmony and the sanctity of human life no matter the place of origin. In this regard David Hume's "is" versus "ought" argument comes to mind. This is interchangeable with the naturalistic fallacy. In some way, shape, or form; the social progress the western world has experienced owes a debt of gratitude to him because where moral development is concerned we can now assert that "might does not make right." Yet Hume's personal assessment of blacks' ability to compete in open social competitions was not a flattering one.

Social interaction is the cornerstone of human life as we learned in the last section and it has been that way long before the noble lie went into effect. Skilled social functioning is a highly complex process that brings together two important features: social psychology and the underlying neuroscience that allows for such skill and social intelligence. To help us understand this, researchers David M. Amodio & Chris D. Firth (2006) consider the factors which underscore this behavior.

> For humans, like many other animals species, survival depends on effective social functioning. Social skills facilitate our access to sustenance, protection, and mates, and socially adept individuals tend to be healthier and live longer.

> Knowledge about the self, perceptions of others, and interpersonal motivations are carefully orchestrated to support skilled social functioning.

> Social psychologists have investigated how the self interacts dynamically with the social environment, and how knowledge structures of social groups (such as stereotypes) might influence behavior through both conscious and unconscious mechanisms.

> Neuroscientists meanwhile have investigated how underlying neural structures support unique yet coordinated roles in various aspects of social cognition.

Let's reconsider for instance the comments of Kati Haycock, president of The Education Trust taken from the *U.S News & World Report* piece. She made an observation that we would all do well to know more about because it is one that keeps appearing across virtually all strata of social life in this country. There is a social cosmology to it that cries out for explanation. And there are now many books that go a long way to explaining that ongoing social cosmology. Steven Pinker's (2002) *"The Blank Slate,"* Tomas Sowell's (1994) *"Race & Culture"* are two. Others include Jared Diamond's (2000) *"Guns, Germs & Steel,"* and *"The 10,000 Year Explosion"* (2010) by Gregory Cochran & Henry Harpending. They all implicate human historical trajectories and what human groups living in disparate did to survive and thrive in disparate regions of the world. To better appreciate the comments of Kati Haycock, and thus to have some idea of how to more aptly approach the challenge she mentioned; one would need to understand something about the specialization process of isolated human group's culture across historical time and its impact in our world presently.

In short, culture is the art of survival. It is the ways in which a group of people have decided to go about fulfilling their physical, material and social needs. In a complex, sophisticated society such as ours; institutions and social and economic systems provide the means to these ends. At its extremes, this is a far cry from the trappings of a hunter/gatherer lifestyle out of which we all came. The cultural space in between those two ways of human survival is sometimes referred to as cultural progress. This is due mostly to the significant amount of life altering advances in technology and innovation humankind has made in the time between that of a hunter/gatherer lifestyle and those human societies that have pioneered ways of putting people on the moon or conducting MRI's and brain imaging to assist in the preservation of life.

The ability to put people on the moon doesn't directly provide for our physical and material needs such as providing food, water and shelter to a human population. But it does speak volumes about the people doing it. In real and undeniable ways it simply takes hugely complex social systems, institutions with a long history of social capital and technological maturity, a talent pool and infrastructure to do so. When we look at the nations with such capabilities, their historical trajectories are illustrative of a population enmeshed in cultural progress and innovation of that sort. We are not likely to find such parallels in sociality, nor a history of cultural, innovative and technological orientations among hunter/gatherer tribes. And generally speaking all of us who inhabit this society possess a lineage that falls somewhere in between these two polarizing ways of being human.

All of this is good to know because it provides the basis for understanding the next section as well as making us aware of the fact that one's cultural orientation cannot readily replace another simply because a population's culture specializes human populations. Also some of the ways in which we go about making distinctions between culture and the mind are misleading because culture and the individual are not isolated entities, but are concurrent, say researchers Sokol & Strout (2007). As E.O. Wilson puts it "there is nothing contradictory in saying that culture arises from human action while human action arises from culture" (1998).

In like manner, cultures of poverty, as an eco-niche, do the same for its adherents. To unravel it we must have an integration of social, neuroscience, evolutionary theory, historical, economic, and cultural studies to understand human actions should we ever hope to affect change.

An intellectual giant of mine C. Wright Mills (1959, 2000) long suspected that "human nature" played an important role in the sociological affairs of individuals and one's sense of peoplehood otherwise known as race. His sociological imagination was to include an understanding of human diversity (p.133). He also bemoaned the manmade divisions academia imposed on the understanding of human behavior; that it functioned more as a hindrance which handicapped our ability to comprehend human actions.

Presciently, Mills understood that all aspects of the human person must be allowed to contribute to understanding human actions when he wrote, "...the idea that the individual can understand his own experience and gauge his own fate only by locating himself within his period, that he can know his own life chances only by becoming aware of all those individuals in his circumstances" (p.5).

For African Americans especially, together with the rest of humankind I can't think of a more astute way of navigating the present social environment because it beckons all individuals to consider the torrents of human history and to also consider what would be some of the harsh realities stemming from the collisions of human groups throughout history and how we are all put upon to figure solutions for it. "In many ways it is a terrible lesson; in many ways a magnificent one" (Mills, C.W. 1959).

****

THE MAKING OF THE MODERN WORLD

If you go back to 1800, everybody was poor. I mean everybody. The Industrial
Revolution kicked in, and a lot of countries benefited, but by no means everyone.

Bill Gates

It has been said that "history is one damn thing after another." Some attribute the saying to a famous historian named Arnold Toynbee and some say it was Winston Churchill. Both hail from England. Today we here in America, as well as the rest of the modern world are living in the shadow of many of those damn things which can also be called starting points, head starts, and accomplishments that ranged across all areas of life both then and now.

European history and especially the history of Great Britain spawned legacies that continue to form the basis to how we understand ourselves and the world around us. What is most important about that activity and the central role it played in the development of the world as we know it is that it cannot be undone. In other words history cannot simply be relegated to being history; not only does it live on, it continues to shape our lives going forward. We are all better off knowing how so; than dwelling in ignorance.

In his book, *"Empire: How Britain Made the Modern World"* (2003), Niall Ferguson chronicles some of the important events in English history which reveals to the reader how a collection of people from a tiny island region became a world empire upon which the sun never sat. The accomplishments of Great Britain and its rise to empire span 200 years and exerted a hegemony that was greater than that of America. One of the vestiges of the British Empire resulted in English becoming the official language of the western world, and where commerce is concerned, the official language of globalization and technology.

Today however, says Niall Ferguson, "The Empire sins tend to be better remembered than its achievements. Yet traveling the world today you keep on encountering the living legacies of Britain's age of Empire. It was British traders who united the world in a single capitalistic economy. While British migration changed the face of whole continents, Protestant Christianity spread from Clapham to Capetown. Western norms of law, order and government were exported too. And parliamentary democracy became the yardstick by which all political systems are judged. These are the pillars of the modern world. And if you like the modern world, you can't deny its debt to the British Empire."

By 1922 the British Empire held sway over one-fifth of world's population and controlled about 25%of the globe's land mass. This resulted in its political, legal, linguistic and cultural legacy becoming so widespread (Wikipedia 2014).

But long before any of that took place, the people who occupied the group of islands which was to become known as the British Isles underwent a vast degree of change in order to arrive at such an exalted place in world affairs. American historian Tomas Sowell (1998) informs us that:

> "For about one-fifth of its recorded history, Britain was a conquered country, a province of the Rome Empire—and one of the more backward provinces at that. Men from other provinces ruled over Britain, but Britons did not rule other provinces. One measure of the backwardness of pre-Roman Britain was the ease with which it was conquered by greatly outnumbered Roman soldiers and held in subjugation... The Romans were simply better equipped and far better organized. In many others ways, the Romans represented a much more advanced civilization than existed in Britain at that point in history. Indeed, after the Romans withdrew from Britain four centuries later, the Britons began to retrogress, and in many respects it was centuries after that before Britain regained the economic, social, or cultural levels it had reached as a province of the Roman Empire" (p.22).

The transformation under which this population of people would rise from such humble beginnings to a foremost world empire has been the subject of many books. That's good because it saves us from having to cover the rise and retirement of the British Empire. What is important for us nonetheless is what we can take from such a sprawling narrative that can be used as pedagogy.

One of the things that were characteristic of not only the people of the British Isles but also Europe as a whole was a thirst for anything that offered a competitive advantage in warfare and economics. On this score, "...Europe's geographical balkanization resulted in dozens or hundreds of independent, competing statelets and centers of innovation. If one state did not pursue some particular innovation, another did, forcing neighboring states to do likewise or else be conquered or left economically behind" (Diamond, J. 1999 p.416). This is illustrative of the kind of open-ended cultural orientation that prevailed throughout European populations. As a result, culture as the art of survival embedded a welcoming atmosphere where innovations, tactics, strategy and new ideas "competed for better and worse ways of getting things done."

In addition a host of other traits involving personality, sociality and cognition would tend to run consistent with that kind of mindset. All of which play a role in what we understand as cultural progress. I mentioned "head starts" earlier. It was out of this kind of beginning; call it an inter-

36

rivalry among Europeans as they scrimmaged for social and economic dominance that provided the basis for progress based explicitly upon competing with other human beings. Today European based societies are not only progressive societies, but are world leaders in the globalization process.

Another major point of departure is that through the progression of time, those once competing statelets and states of Europe evolved ways of increasing the level of cooperation among themselves, while suppressing highly disruptive competitions that littered their history. This created a spirit of cooperation amongst themselves, and a greater recognition of themselves as a biological and cultural racial population as the exploration of world brought them into contact with human populations in distant regions of the world.

Another key feature is trust. Political scientist Francis Fukuyama (1995) has shown that economic life as well as a nation's wellbeing and "its ability to compete, is conditioned by a single, pervasive cultural characteristic: the level of trust inherent in the society." In his book *"Trust: the social virtues and the creation of prosperity"* Fukuyama brilliantly explains how social capital arose among Europeans and European based societies leading to a network of high-trust societies. The benefits of which run on and on in so far as "[e]conomic life represents a crucial part of social life and is knit together by a wide variety of norms, rules, moral obligations and other habits that together shape the society" (p.7).

Elsewhere Max Weber (1864-1920) was a German sociologist. He too is also considered one of the founding fathers of sociology. He is noted for the thesis he presented in *"The Protestant Ethic and the Spirit of Capitalism"* (1930) which describes how capitalism in Northern Europe evolved out of a Calvinist ethic that shaped how its adherents engaged in work in the secular world. They developed businesses, and established trades as a means of accumulating wealth for investment. Among the believers, the accumulation of wealth and its preservation was seen as a way of determining the measure of God's favor in the interim where the religious doctrine of predestination ruled. The Protestant work ethic became an ever increasing economic force that embedded the unintentional mass action of a population that influenced the development of capitalism that in time would spread around the globe.

These are but a few of the many ways in which seminal ideas and innovations which got their start in Europe had in time come to define what is means to be human. Within such a social environment, "Human survival depends on cultural conformity, which requires that every individual become a specialist, be committed to a few values, and acquire knowledge and skill of a single society" (Spradley & McCurdy 1987).

But it's not just values that determine success from failure. People who are held captive by a culture of poverty actually want and value much of what those who are not captives want and desire. Part of the disconnect between them centers around the possession of "culturally-shaped skills, habits, and styles" writes American sociologist Ann Swidler (1986). Swindler says that "people may share common aspirations, while remaining profoundly different in the way their culture organizes their overall pattern of behavior." What's more, cultural organization very much involves a person's sense of self as they evaluate the socio-cultural world around them. That sense of self cannot be highly discordant with one's future self, given that it takes a level of confidence to strive toward that goal within the specifics of a cultural orientation. Thus it takes a cultural competency or literacy given that "to adopt a line of conduct, one needs an image of the kind of world in which one is trying to act, a sense that one can read reasonably accurately (through one's own feelings and through the responses of others) how one is doing, and a capacity to choose among alternative lines of action" (Swindler, A. 1986). Thus the making of the modern world and its propagation was very much a cultural crucible which sculpted a relatively isolated population of people over a significant expanse of time.

****

HOW "WHITENESS" CAME TO BE

A lot of our work could be called "genetic history." ...we, however, are interested in the historical factors that have influenced natural selection in humans, particularly those having to do with the creation and spread of new, favorable alleles.

Cochran & Harpending

It doesn't take a major leap to understand how a population of people that have spent a considerable amount of time in relative social isolation can over time come to resemble each other not only in appearance but also in biology and cultural outlook especially where culture is the art of survival. Today the biology of race can be established on genetic basis alone (Sarich & Miele 2004; Rowe, D.C. 2005; Cochran & Harpending 2010).

For the longest time it was held and hoped that the concept of race was meaningless. Many thought that once significant social barriers were removed; longstanding racial populations that suffered mightily throughout recent history would exhibit a jail break mentality toward actualizing the personal freedom their forefathers had long since given up any hope of ever knowing. Currently however something other than that is taking place. In fact the converse seems more the reality as "people who are free to behave differently from one another in the important daily affairs of life inevitably generate the social and economic inequalities that equalitarianism seeks to suppress" (Herrnstein & Murray 1994).

Race is not a meaningless concept neither in its biology nor cultural regime. Both have a major impact across all aspects of life. Over the last 10,000 years of human existence more racial divergence has taken place within our species than at any other time since the inception of *Homo sapiens* (Cochran & Harpending 2010). "Not only has *Homo sapiens* been doing some major genetic reshuffling since our species formed, but the rate of human evolution may, if anything, have increased... we continue to show genetically induced changes in our physiology and perhaps in our behavior as well. Until fairly recently in our history, human races in various parts of the world were becoming more rather than less distinct. Even today the conditions of modern life could be driving changes to genes for certain behavioral traits" says University of Washington biologist Peter Ward (2013).

Over the course of the last 10,000 years humankind has initiated several very important changes in how we go about providing for our needs and using the earth resources as a means to do so. The first important change took place with the creation and spread of agriculture. The transition from hunter/gatherers to agriculture (aka "farmer power") (Diamond, J. 1999) gave those populations who were able to flourish with it the ability to free themselves from the burden of being so closely tied to the land. For instance a farm that is tended to by a farming family can establish and maintain herds of livestock and exploit a few acres of nutrient dense soil to produce a substantial amount of food.

Whereas hunter/gatherer tribes can only expand their numbers in direct proportion to what they are able to provide through hunting and gathering, farmer power facilitates increases in population leading to population density. Another chief advantage of farming is the ability to create food surpluses and storage.

As a result, large, population dense and socially stratified societies arose. In time new developments in technologies emerged such as steel. Among its many uses, the making of swords for fighting was one of them. Together with guns, shipbuilding technologies and navigation skills; for those populations that were fortunate enough to settle in geographically ideal locations around the world; they would experience a head start that conferred a competitive advantage in competing with other populations for the earth's resources and its people (Diamond, J. 1999).

And in terms of social stratification and the evolution of mind, people have a natural tendency to organize themselves in a way that begets social class. "I would claim that the existence of a hierarchy or system of rank is a near-universal tendency. There are very few human societies without differences in social status, and when attempts are made to abolish such differences they tend to re-emerge quite rapidly" says Peter Singer (2000) a professor of bioethics at Princeton University. It followed naturally that with changes in the way those populations went about meeting their needs and orienting themselves in the social world; consistent with the transition from hunting and gathering to agriculture, meaningful transitions took place in sociality, political organization, language and writing that was consistent with the degree of complexity evolving ecological and social environments presented.

And while it's true that there are older civilizations than those of Europe located in the Middle East and Asia, much of what it took to make the modern world happened as a result of the pan-European world appropriating technologies and innovations that began among those older civilizations. The difference maker in terms of competitiveness was that somewhere along their historical trajectory something occurred to halt their cultural progress. In an introduction to "World-System Analysis" (2004) Immanuel Wallerstein elaborates on the distinctions.

The world was however made up of more than just the "modern" states and these so-called primitive peoples. These were large regions outside the pan-European zone which was called in the nineteenth century a "high civilization"—for example, China, India, Persia, the Arab World. All these zones had certain common characteristic: writing; a dominant language which was used in the writing... All these zones had been in the past, and sometimes continued to be even in the present, the location of bureaucratic "world empires" that had embraced large areas, and therefore developed a common language, a common religion, and many other common customs. This is what was meant when they were called "high civilizations." These regions all shared another feature in the nineteenth century. They were no longer as strong militarily or technologically as the pan-European world. So the pan-European world considered that they were not "modern." Still, their inhabitants clearly did not meet the description of "primitive" peoples, even by pan-European standards (p.8).

So the transition from hunter/gatherer to agriculture was an event that diverged the world's people in significant ways. Building upon what had already taken place in the world as a result of the first transition; another major shift in human activity took place as the industrial revolution spread across parts of Europe. Specifically the Western world would undergo a transformation spanning a time frame of 1650 to the 1800s that would place them a great distance ahead of the rest of the world in terms of cultural progress. "During the eighteenth century English mechanics and scientists had developed spinning and weaving devices driven by water and later by steam engines that dramatically increased yarn and textile production. Their machines attracted little fanfare or attention at first. In time, however, this revolution, even more than the revolution in France, reshaped the human condition" (Andrea & Overfield 1998).

In the 18th century, seminal innovations in science also known as "the Enlightenment" spearheaded breakthroughs in how we understand the natural world around us. These novel epiphanies of human life lifted Europe out of the dark ages: the period of intellectual, economic regression and despair that followed the collapse of the Roman Empire. Individuals at the forefront of this era that reshaped the human condition were such individuals as the Polish astronomer Nicholas Copernicus (1473-1543) and his contribution "On the Revolutions of the Heavenly Spheres," Galileo Galilei (1564-1642) the Italian scientist who laid the foundations of modern physics and astronomy, and the English physicist and mathematician Isaac Newton (1642-1727) who laid the foundations of classical mechanics. There was the Frenchman Rene Descartes (1539-1650), and the English thinker Francis Bacon (1561-1626) whose contributions established the rules and methods of science. And some posit that the greatest idea anyone ever had was Darwin's grand idea of evolution by natural selection (Charles Darwin 1809-1882).

This is not meant to be summa on European history. But it is meant to offer us some idea of the cultural progress which took place there and in so doing it changed or "specialized" those populations which took part in it and as well all those that lived in its wake. Europe during this time period and even prior to it was at the center of much conflict and expansion. Yet the march toward an ever evolving civil society never ceased as the march of modernity itself was unrelenting.

Concepts such as civilization or modernity, at bottom are a way in which a group of people have sought to organize social, political and economic life. Thus these concepts are synonymous with the word culture: as the art of survival. Everything starting with the advent of agriculture to the industrial revolution and beyond informs us of what can be understood as white culture or whiteness. A civil society means "a complex welter of intermediate institutions, including businesses, voluntary associations, educational institutions, clubs, unions, media, charities, and churches—[which] builds, in turn, on the family, the primary instrument by which people are socialized into their culture and given the skills that allow them to live in broader society and through which the values and knowledge of that society are transmitted across the generations" (Fukuyama, F 1995).

A civil society cannot exist absent the rule of law, either as codified law or as something a population does that can be best described by the rule of law. The British historian Niall Ferguson mentioned that "Western norms of law, order and government were exported." Clearly there is not much about America that is not an offshoot of Britain's age of empire. This extends to the individuals that settled America originally of whom American culture is indicative. "The United States was settled primarily by Britain and inherited not just British law but British culture as well" (Fukuyama, F. 1999).

Historically as well as currently it follows then that those individuals whose heritage is steeped in European history would on average enjoy a competitive advantage given their background capacities. Also European history is a lot longer in the tooth than just Britain's age of empire. It spans more than 10,000 years. During that time their social evolution exerted a selection pressure upon genotype that produced phenotype. Professor John Searle (1995) of University of California Berkeley can help us understand the impact of it in contemporary society.

> I am saying if you understand the complexity of the causation involved, you can see that often the person who behaves in a skillful way within an institution behaves as if he were following the rules, but not because he is following the rules unconsciously nor because his behavior is caused by an undifferentiated mechanism that happens to look as if it were rule structured, but rather because the mechanism had evolved precisely so that it will be sensitive to the rules.

... the point is that we should not say that the man who is at home in his society, the man who is chez lui in the social institution of the society, is at home because he has mastered the rules of his society, but rather that the man has developed a set of capacities and abilities that render him at home in the society... (p. 147)

"Whiteness" at its height is a specialization; a descent with modifications both in biology and culture that has been conferred to those individuals whose heritage traces directly back to those human populations that took part in the making of the modern world. What is more, it goes back further than just the making of the modern world given that those who made the modern world, were among the first to develop agriculture and reaped the benefits of a head start through the experience.

Throughout American history and even today whiteness confers a social advantage or privilege all others have had to work toward. That social advantage can be best understood by way of this comparison: *"Prospects for world domination of sub-Saharan Africans, Aboriginal Australians, and Native Americans remain dim. The hand of history's course at 8,000 B.C. lies heavily on us"* (Diamond, J. 1999).

****

WORKING TOWARD WHITENESS

I AM white, I have spent years studying what it means to be white in a society that proclaims race is meaningless, yet is deeply divided by race. This is what I have learned: Any white person living in the United States will develop opinions about race simply by swimming in the water of our culture.

Robin DiAngelo

The story of the United States can be told in a variety of ways. So much has taken place here since its inception. To continue the narrative that informs the theme of this book, we would want to know something about the continuity between Europe, specifically Britain and America as the United States. At the outset, these two locales and the individuals which comprised them were at one time so tightly intertwined that it took a Declaration of Independence and the American War of Independence to separate the two.

But while the people of the 13 colonies were successful in gaining their independence and the right to determine their own destiny, they did so with the cultural orientations, world views and sense of self that was still European in some important ways. There was no reinvention of the wheel in these areas. Why was that?

I think that unlike many of the collisions that took place across human history, this one was rather unique in that while they sought political and economic freedom, they were equal in intellect to those of whom they demanded their freedom from. And that was probably a determining factor in why they succeeded at winning their bid for freedom. Many of the founding fathers were polymaths. They were products of the age of science and the Enlightenment. In short, "[t]he modern United States is a European molded society" (Diamond, J. 1999).

Once the dust settled from the war, the founding fathers had covered major ground "to form a more perfect union." The story of America can also be told from the standpoint of its open borders. "Immigration has shaped the contours of this nation's history from its founding to the present day. Immigration has shaped this nation's cities, its institutions, industries, and laws, its literature and its culture" says research professor Sidney Verba of Harvard University (http://tiny.cc/0zj7sx)

America was to become a melting pot; a place where diverse human populations could come and make their way in the world. Out of many; one—but the pot into which those immigrating groups were poured was itself molded according to a standard. That standard served as the benchmark on how to succeed at life in America.

Milton Gordon (1964) was an American sociologist who studied assimilation in American life. For Milton, writing in the 1960's, one of the things he observed was the ways in which those who were white in every nuance of the concept were unaware of whiteness as a cultural identity. For this population there was no such thing as "white culture," just a social criterion that could be characterized as being normal.

Milton observed "...the white Protestant American is rarely conscious of the fact that he inhabits a group at all. He inhabits America. The others live in groups."

Even still today "white culture" remains an elusive concept. In an essay, Judith H. Katz captures this well:

> "Where's the value in talking about that? It's so ephemeral, intangible, complex. How can you get your arm around it? It's hard to see, particularly if you're white. ... Therefore, looking at and making explicit what is white culture presents many challenges. More often it's easier to see another person's culture than one's own because our culture is like the air we breathe: it's just there." (pps.k12or.us/files)

What is more, not only is it "just there," it is still advantageous to be specialized at it due to the fact that our social, economic and political institutions are established upon it. Those with such a cultural literacy possess "a significant evolutionary advantage in that they entered a world replete with the ideas, and products of those who have gone before them; they do not have to build the word anew. People form bonds with others, help others, depend on others, compare themselves to others, learn from others, teach others, and experience themselves and the world through the images, ideas, representations, and language of others. Such social influence is both a product and a producer of human nature..." (Markus, H. 2008).

By contrast, all other immigrant populations who arrived upon our shores sporting their own brand of ethnicity and/or racial otherness were put upon with the notion of "working their way toward whiteness." And as the story goes, worked they did because first and foremost we humans have a need to belong and to seek approval from others whom we deem important (Fiske, S. 2010). Being strangers in a new land meant applying a work ethic and getting to know the path by which one could get their immediate needs met. It also meant instilling in younger generations the idea that they can experience upward social mobility and in doing so find social acceptance. Expressions of human achievement that were perhaps near impossible in their country of origin. For them that was assimilation in American life.

45

Back in the day, most individuals' knowledge of what constituted a racial population was not as mature as ours today. Gregor Johann Mendel (1822-1884) the founder of the modern science genetics gained fame posthumously. In those early days prior to Mendel, rarely did anyone let a botched interpretation of what constituted a racial population stand in their way. This is seen in the following illustration. "Fairchild allowed that the new immigrants were 'for the most part white skinned but they were generally regarded as inferior.'" Such immigrants held jobs "Americans" avoided. In all of this, they were "like the negro." But as Fairchild concluded: "the judgment was provisional and the scrutiny would be extended: 'if he proves himself a man and ... acquires wealth and cleans himself up—very well, we might receive him in a generation or two. But at present he is far beneath us, and the burden of proof rests with him'" (Roediger, D. 2005 p.58). This was a time when even among other white individuals privilege was transactional.

Furthermore the social, economic and political institutions that form the bedrock of our society encompasses the history as well as the relentlessness of modernity that makes competitors of us all regardless of race. But a head start is indeed a head start. On average it made and makes "the burden of proof" an uneven social process. Though there have been times in our recent history, as well as in some cases now, where to be white is a social disadvantage. But those are the exceptions not the rule.

Notwithstanding that the "burden of proof" or the fulfillment of important life tasks as understood by those who had set the rules of the game is amplified in the comments of the famous Russian author Fyodor Dostoevsky (1821-1881) when he asked this question on the nature and origins of white culture. "Why, everything, unquestionably almost everything that we have—of development, science, art, civic-mindedness, humanity—everything comes from there, from that same land of holy wonders! Why, our entire life, even from very childhood itself, had been set up along European lines." ("Notes from Underground" p. xi). It was in this fashion that "otherness" meant a working toward whiteness.

****

RACIAL IN-BETWEENESS

Many of the most important decisions ever made about us depend on how strangers see our talents, abilities, and other characteristics.

Robert H. Frank

True of American history, race does embed a power differential. We saw that in the observation made by Jared Diamond. It is as Toni Morrison explained: "race" has functioned as a "metaphor" necessary to the "construction of American-ness". In the creation of our national identity, "American" has been defined as "white" (Takaki, R 1993).

Dostoevsky was talking about life in Russia. But he may as well been talking about life in America; because what he observed serves to explain a metaphorical "melting pot," that melted all other immigrant groups to that reality here in our society. "*Self*ways—ways of seeing, thinking, feeling, and being in the world" (Markus, H. 2008); those who were socially dominant experienced the highest levels of independence and sense of belonging. By contrast, there is "otherness" or those who live in groups. For them, given that the social world was readymade for them as well. Their selfways was an interdependent way of being, in which one's sense of agency and belonging "is more relational or conjoined... organized by the thoughts, feelings, and actions of others in a relationship" says psychologist Hazel Markus of Stanford University.

So is there such a thing as "racial in-betweeness?" The short answer is no. But to answer that question more precisely. One needs an understanding of evolutionary theory and the overview of individual difference that it offers. Also the answer will come encumbered with a few important caveats. Because in everyday life, most of us have a sense that there can be something about an individual or group of individuals which gives the impression of racial in-betweeness.

Charles Darwin (1871) offered the world a way of understanding human variation when he wrote, "There are no races without transition to others; that every race exhibits within itself variations of color, of hair, of feature, and of form, to such a degree as to bridge over to a large extent the gap that separates it from other races. It is asserted that no race is homogenous; that there is a tendency to vary."

In this way racial in-betweeness can take place in the form of obvious physical differences or with something phenotypically different about an individual in personality traits, temperament, sociality, or intelligence which puts the person on par with a population which seems somewhat distal to his own heritage, race or sense of peoplehood. The title of this work is a clear example. As explained by Darwin, most times, the idea of phenotypical overlap is a matter of degree dependent upon what trait is being observed at the time.

Recall this quote. "The choice of becoming a black intellectual is an act of self-imposed marginality in the black community; it assures a peripheral status in and to the black community" (West, C. 1994). That insight suggests to us that this person's sense of belonging is shaped and influenced by the presence of two cultural orientations and literacies. He is conscious of both in terms of selfways and for sure he is confident about his personal self; yet his collective/group identity cross-cuts his personal social identity affecting how he's perceived and to whom (in terms of peoplehood) does he belong.

Thus the dilemma is presented in this fashion, as he moves toward one bona fide self-way; in some important ways, he diverges from another. If in private, relaxed conversation among friends one might find it best or easy to describe him as an Oreo; it comes across as racial in-betweeness.

This does not mean that racial categories don't exist (or that they are infinitely malleable). They do. And sometimes some aspects of racial differences, though they can be minor, in fact can bring forth significant differences when seen from group to group. What's more we can only understand the example above from the standpoint of two data points which gives way to fuller representations of racial categories. In this case, African Americans and Caucasians and the amount of polarity endemic to the two cultures

Today, in the age of human genomics, we now know that the world's human populations can be understood as belonging to one of three racial super hubs: African, Caucasian and Asian. (Balaresque, P.L. et al. 2007; Rowe, D.C. 2005). And it's true that many individuals can trace their lineage back to more than just one of these super hubs, just like all humans on the planet today can be traced back to Africa in the form of mitochondria Eve (Stix, G. 2013). What makes trajectories of human history vital to understand is the stuff (human actions and niche building) which took place in the spaces delineating these points in historical time and the consequences which followed. Because "One of the surprising consequences of the modern version of the Darwinian Theory," writes Richard Dawkins (2006), "is that apparently trivial tiny influences on survival can have a major impact on evolution" (p.4). For our purposes here, what we want out of this is an individual's sense of peoplehood. Our sense of peoplehood, our heritage makes up a fundamental part of our sense of self, our social identity and our possible "future" selves still today.

Historically, the persons who were understood as being racially in-between were immigrant groups such as the Irish, Italians, Jews, and Polish. As explained to us by the whiteness gatekeeper "Fairchild" granted that "for the most part, they were white skinned." These were the immigrants with a chance at working their way toward whiteness. Privilege produces hierarchy and can be resistant to change. It is "organized in ways that encouraged people to use difference to include or exclude, reward or punish, credit or discredit, elevate or oppress, value or devalue, leave alone or harass" (Johnson, A.J. 1997).

But social progress had taken place from the early days of Fairchild to the time of Gordon Milton writing in the 1960s as the once racial in-betweeness of Caucasian populations were more accurately understood as the same in racial population, just ethnically set apart. "In practice, it is probable that these discrete categories are attached to the self not separately or serially but in combination. Our conventional language of ethnic identification within the nation suggests as much. This American is a white Protestant Anglo-Saxon; that one is an Irish Catholic (white race understood), this one is a Negro Protestant (African background understood), that one is a Russian Jew (white race understood). This is the way we identify each other and ourselves when we think, ethnically, about Who We Are within the national boundaries. These are the labels of grouphood which history made sure would eventually be attached to our psychological self as we arrived in the world within the confines of this family rather than that one" (p.26).

****

RACE: IN BINARY TERMS

While white Americans recognized the existence of many "racial" groups which did not fit easily into this binary system of categorization, this did not prevent them from viewing African Americans as a central paradigm of racial "otherness."

Eric L. Goldstein, *The Price of Whiteness: Jews, Race, and American Identity*

What I would like to do here is not to rehash the history of Africans/African-Americans in this nation; mostly because just about all of us already know the history. If immigrant groups which evinced some semblance of otherness experienced social oppression and prejudice premised on difference, then think of that to the tenth power when thinking about the degree of social isolation and degradation experienced by those who were brought here in chains. In short they were not considered human.

What I'd prefer to do is offer some sense of the social progress that has taken place in contemporary America since that time by first discussing that ignoble beginning in terms of human belongingness and what "otherness" means. Then turn to what I think is a more pertinent discussion for the here and now.

Notably, something socially seismic happened the night this nation elected Barack Obama as the 44th President of the United States. "We the people," in an official sense, went from a society which since its inception was explicitly built upon dominance and centered squarely upon race; to a society based on prestige where knowledge, skill, expertise and individual effort could matter more than someone's heritage in defining individual achievement. The truth of the matter is that such individual freedom was already largely in play before that night. Nonetheless, on that night, by electing Barack Obama, this nation was able to demonstrate that it is truly capable of looking at the content of one's character over and above the color of one's skin. And maybe it's just me, but the impression I got was that this triumph was an American accomplishment not just one limited to a political party. That event accomplished a feat of social inclusiveness this nation had been striving for since the great cultural revolutions of the 1960s.

To go from a place in this nation where a person of our President's likeness was once considered only three-fifths of a person to a place where persons of "his kind of otherness" can experience the sense of belongingness and ethical consideration afforded all other socially accepted persons across American history did not come easy. Social progress was and still is dynamic and uneven and it can take on trends with the potential to reverse itself.

Comparatively, while Blacks in the Western world experienced huge deficits in human dignity due to a deeply entrenched racial prejudice and the stickiness of racial otherness, the notion of racial in-betweeness that had historically placed some Caucasian populations outside of that category came to be understood as such. But while human genetic diversity giving way to human racial populations adheres to patterns of selection in geography, pathogens, climate, dietary and cognitive adaptations the further upstream one goes (Balaresque, P.L. et al. 2007). Human history, at the same time is replete with competitions and collisions and the consequences of them. This had led to human hierarchy.

On the world stage as well as in America, racial otherness always reflected that hierarchy. Historically here was the layout that reveals to us Blacks as a "paradigm of racial otherness."

> 'Races' formed an evolutionary hierarchy with Europeans at the top and, at the bottom, other peoples, such as, for example, indigenous Australians, South African 'Bushmen' and South American Indians. In this scheme, intermediate rankings varied, but Africans were always low, while Chinese and Indians jostled, as it were, for silver and bronze metal placings. Much could be said about this but a few points must suffice. First, physically the human evolutionary process was widely held to have been finished and Europeans to have effectively won. Second, 'civilization' was seen as a sort of natural phenomenon, the pinnacle of evolutionary development. European superiority was not therefore seen as *cultural* but as *natural*. The white European was, by virtue of his (definitely!) evolutionary superiority, the vehicle and model by which this essentially natural progression had been accomplished. Third, 'lower races' were thus in diverse states of 'arrested development', in evolutionary dead-ends from which escape was impossible without white aid, if at all (levels of optimism differed) ("Putting Psychology in its Place," Richards, G. 2002).

Like the author stipulated *"Much could be said about this."* And while I have to stay within the confines of this discussion, one of my long range goals as a mere student of evolutionary theory is to delve more deeply into how the social world and human relations could be construed in such ways. How are we to understand such things presently in the age of human genomics, neuroscience and the gene-culture coevolutionary process and a continuing social cosmology that seem to confirm those findings where the world's Black/African populations are concerned? I will do all that I can in forth coming submissions to help our understanding of it all. But for now, the one thing I will call your attention to is the last-place-ness of African populations.

Throughout the last 10,000 years of human history that has been the fate of such people (Diamond, J. 1999). That harsh reality has had some very deeply ingrained consequences upon that population and their life chances moving forward. The one salient thing about being perceived as a paradigm of racial otherness is the amount of psychological distancing foisted upon those with that stigma. It was tantamount to social death: a transactional social experience between those with power and privilege and the absolutely powerless. It's been observed that social death has the potential to utterly transform the human person both externally and more importantly internally (Patterson, O. 1982). It changes the way such people view themselves by aligning their sense of self-worth and "how" they belong in the social environment in which they find themselves.

The kind of "racial otherness" which leads to the social death experienced by Africans/African Americans across the span of recent human history has known no equal. And surprisingly, by ignoring or remaining willfully ignorant about the long-term consequences of such human interaction, it allows for its continuation in the contemporary world. Such an understanding cannot be had without an understanding of human nature which respects the modern version of Darwinian theory (Dawkins, R. 2006), (Singer, P. 2000).

In our world today otherness is what we see all around us in being a nation of immigrants. We are a highly diverse human society. And we still use otherness in very significant ways to assist us in navigating the social world. We do this because: "The concept of 'otherness' is also integral to the comprehending of a person, as people construct roles for themselves in relation to an 'other' as part of a process of reaction that is not necessarily related to stigmatization or condemnation. Otherness is imperative to national identities, where practices of admittance and segregation can form and sustain boundaries and national character. Otherness helps distinguish between home and away, the uncertain and certain. It often involves the demonization and dehumanization of groups, which further justifies attempts to civilize and exploit these 'inferior' others" (http://lmtowton.wordpress.com/tag/otherness/).

So we really should not kid ourselves about how we don't see human differences when it's all around us. It is instrumental to skilled social functioning that we make such observations. But as Eric L. Goldstein informed us in the opening to this section, seeing otherness in African Americans and the vast degree of psychological distancing it created among the two human populations in question; to this day, it is still something that requires examination and mindfulness due to the consequences which followed. But a new kind of examination and mindfulness, one that departs greatly from the animosity and polarizing stance of old—even though the impetus for such problems are the products of history.

In one sense, there will always be challenges to human interaction. That is no reason to think that a day will come which will carry us full circle allowing for the harmonious existence of tens of billions of people on a planet with limited and dwindling resources. As one evolutionary theorist puts it, "at no point in the history of Homo sapiens, therefore, is there any reason to believe that we were perfect creatures in perfect harmony with either our environment or with each another. Knowledge of our past may be invaluable for understanding the present and for planning the future but there is no returning to a golden age that never was" (Barkow, J. 2002).

Nonetheless, thank God for social progress or thank humankind for the ability to vary and to evolve sociologically. Peter Singer of Princeton University knows something of the latter and in a contribution to help us understand how human societies have evolved to be more ethically inclusive of human diversity. His theory of the expanding circle of moral inclusiveness describes how Western societies have experienced transitions by extending ethically to others. It began with something as small as the family unit, moved to include one's tribe, one's race, the human race, the animals of the earth and to the earth itself.

Therefore, while we cannot return to a golden age that never was, we have proven that at least we can approximate it. Recall Dostoevsky's comments about how our lives are arranged along European lines? Here is an example, one of prosociality that is hard to find fault with. Standing on the shoulders of W.E.H. Lecky (1838-1903) and his contribution, *The History of European Morals,*" Peter Singer (1981) offers us this piece from that contribution. "The moral unity to be expected in different ages is not a unity of standard, or of acts, but a unity of tendency... At one time the benevolent affections embrace merely the family, soon the circle expanding includes first a class, then a nation, then a coalition of nations, then all humanity, and finally, its influence is felt in the dealings of man with the animal world."

Lastly, "we all have the ability to use 'difference' or 'otherness' to include or exclude..." Yet somehow through the matriculation of Western ethics into the affairs of humankind as well as its ability to extend to others who were traditionally outside that circle of moral inclusiveness—that circle of moral inclusiveness now includes the greatest of all sociological outliers, those of whom that were thought of as the "paradigm of racial otherness," African Americans.

But prosocial human interactions and the sense of belongingness we derived from it requires something of positive social worth from all participants involved. It's transactional like "I'm okay; you're okay" but for the broader society. Anything less than prosocial interactions polarize human groups and tend to produce negative effects in psychosocial health, undermining what it means to be human.

Belongingness researchers Roy F. Baumeister and Mark R. Leary (1995) suspect that "if belongingness is indeed a fundamental human need, then reactions to a loss of belongingness should go beyond negative affect to include some type of pathology. People who are socially deprived should exhibit a variety of ill effects, such as signs of maladjustment or stress, behavioral or psychological pathology, and possibly health problems. *They should also show an increase in goal-directed activity aimed at forming relationships"* (p. 500).

****

ACTING WHITE

Obama said that it is important for Americans to know their roots and where they come from, but not be held hostage by our cultures from advancing in life. Then Obama got real. He talked about how black Americans use this "group think" psychology to bully other blacks, keep them from expressing themselves as individuals and stop them from assimilating into the broader culture of America.

Crystal Wright

To continue with the preface that closed out the last section. Simply put, it is not a health promoting fixture of humanness to live with a constant social stigma. Humans have a need to belong and to feel acceptable to themselves and to other individuals in their social environment. We crave social acceptance, acknowledgement and positive reinforcement and in these ways we find dignity and meaning in life among those we find ourselves in the midst of. Generally speaking, when people find themselves in highly tenuous social circumstances they "strive to reduce feelings of uncertainty about themselves, their social world and their place within it— they like to know who they are and how to behave, and who others are and how they might behave. Being properly located in this way renders the social world and one's place within it relatively predictable and allows one to plan effective action, avoid harm, know who to trust, and so forth" (Hogg, M.A. et al. 2005).

Therefore, without question, one of the most socially paralyzing, debilitating and self-defeating notions Black America has ever devised against itself is the slander of the notion of "acting white." Generally speaking, acting white concerns itself with communicating as to make oneself understood; simply speaking English; and taking the time to better oneself educationally to increase one's life chances in a complex society. The introduction gave us a portrait of the idea and how it's perceived both by mainstream America to whom it makes all the sense in the world and to the preponderance of African Americans to whom it's just an act.

It was Victor Frankl (2006) who once wrote that "an abnormal reaction to an abnormal situation is normal behavior." Frankl (1905-1997) was someone who knew firsthand what it felt like to have one's dignity eviscerated. A European Jew, during his lifetime he suffered and survived the concentration camps of Nazi Germany. Concerning his observation though, I often pondered the many ways in which that could be true. For instance if a population of people were to spend centuries enduring subjugation; what would be some of the lingering effects leading toward situations where the abnormal is normal regarding the need to belong?

One thing is for sure, prisons of the mind or social prisons are much more difficult to come to terms with than captives who are merely freed from that which restrains them physically such as a jail cell or prison bars. Examples such as PTSD, difficulty forming positive social bonds, and maladaptive adult attachments are a few instances where this is true. Specifically, research has shown that even when a marriage terminates in divorce, often times the relationship doesn't end, it merely changes. That some form of attachment often lingers on even though it is shot through with ambivalence (Vaughan, D. 1986).Moreover, "The unwillingness to leave an abusive intimate partner is another manifestation of the strength of the need to belong and of the resulting reluctance to break social bonds. The fact people resist breaking off an attachment that causes pain attests to how deeply rooted and powerful the need to belong is" (Baumeister & Leary 1995).

The hope is that by now we are beginning to get a grasp of how complex human relations can be even when many individuals seem to prefer to operate in the self-delusion that there can be two Americas: one deemed "Black America" and the other being all other Americans who comprise mainstream American society. In principle, that was supposed to be the lesson learned in dismantling "the separate but equal" sociological paradigm of racial interaction. To put it another way, it didn't work when racial segregation was a consequence of law and social norms. It still doesn't work when it is achieved through of some de facto, naturalistic manner.

What Herman Melville observed about human belongingness and our interconnectivity to other human beings in our social environment maintains its integrity even in those instances when it may be the abiding hope of some that it wouldn't. For Black America there is an important learning curve to be overcome here. Frankl in his "search for meaning" believed that a life driven by purpose and examination was a life elevated by the process of doing so. To that end he wrote, "life ultimately means taking the responsibility to find the right answer to its problems and to fulfill the tasks which it constantly sets for each individual" (p.77).

In the quote which closed the last section belongingness researchers cited a number of mental, social and societal ills which plague those who live with a significant degree of social isolation. All of those things plague the African American community. Yet the last item they mentioned is something which is conspicuously absent among this group as they abide in contemporary America. In fact the converse is more true of this population. A number of important trends suggest that African Americans are becoming more socially isolated in contemporary society and the consequences are disastrous. Paradoxically in some ways, as a group, black Americans are worse off now than they were a half century ago.

This is somewhat perplexing because the history of blacks in America is fraught with the tribulations associated with making strides toward social acceptance and a greater sense of dignity. The civil rights movement of the 1960s and social gains which came out of that activity has been abdicated and mostly abandoned. In a somewhat bizarre way it has become fashionable to flaunt just how socially distal one's behavior and manner of dress can be in an apparent attempt to reject the mores of civil society. Even when it's to their own detriment; and that's just the beginning.

Researchers seeking to better understand human behavior in the age of genomics are beginning to realize that race intersects and plays a role in the etiology of disease. That at the confluence of genetics, biology, society, culture, intra-psychic experiences, and behavior; race cannot so easily be dismissed as meaningless (Bonham, V.L. et al. 2005). Specifically "racially identified minority groups such as people of African descent may have cultural behavioral patterns that reflect not only their culture but also a social and political reaction to a history of prejudice and discrimination" (Wang & Sue 2005).

Okay, most people can understand that. It's just that there is something which comes across as abnormal about the current arrangement when compared to that of the older generations of African Americans who came of age in the 1960s. They yearned for greater social acceptance and with it dignity. They lived at a time when real racial animus was both flagrant and tangible. Yet they fought nonviolently, suffered false arrest, beatings, lynching, and public shaming to obtain the very thing so easy abdicated by the generations of today. If anyone had just cause to shrug off being socially accepted, it should have been them. Not the generations of today where individual freedom is boundless compared to the era of the 1960's. It is in that sense that I think about how an abnormal reaction to an abnormal situation can become normal behavior. "Normal behavior" because those who engage in prosociality, seek social capital and aspire to compete in open social competitions where individuals rise and fall on their merit and tenacity are seen as abnormal; as "acting white." In fact we could go so far as to say that their behavior is adaptive or "normal" should we evaluate it from the standpoint of the last point made by Baumeister & Leary at the close out the last section.

There is a real dilemma here because it seems as if Blacks in contemporary America have more of a connection to the past than those of older generations. The social past is an important factor in the lives of us all and in some ways it seems to come down to how one is willing to proceed in light of the past.

This is a pivotal point because "[p]astness [a population's historical trajectory] is a mode by which persons are persuaded to act in the present. Such historical guidelines possess the potential of making individuals act in ways they otherwise might not" says Immanuel Wallerstein (p.301). But more may be said about this. Because past generations of African Americans did not have an option due to the nature of the social environment, they were consigned against their will to an ignoble social station. Today one can't help but think that that past-ness is being used to legitimize failure also known as "black failure." The portent can be further understood by the correlation that with increasing social isolation comes a more precarious situation for those who are isolated. If anything is absolute it is that fact.

In scientific psychology today there is much which tells us that the members of our modern society cannot live for themselves. Where human belongingness is concerned we humans tend to define humanness by the humans around us. I think it was Dostoevsky who said that "consciousness is suffering" and an awareness of relative deprivation in one's life can spawn a host of decrements in health, and life contentment leading to hopelessness and suicide ideation (Marmot, M. 2004). From the discipline of comparative psychology, noted primatologist Fran de Waal of Emory University agrees that "evolution has instilled a need to belong and feel accepted" (2005, p. 235). With belongingness being basic to our species (Fiske, S. 2002), scholars seek "to understand how evolution has shaped this core need in us and how the behavior of modern humans is constrained by it" (Levine & Kerr 2007).

Because belongingness is basic to our species, what studies in human deprivation tell us is that "the mind is a relevance making machine" and "despite the widespread belief that molecular biology will soon vanquish disease, there remains the discomforting fact that health can be predicted to an astonishing extent by being poor, *feeling* poor, and being *made* to feel poor..." says Stanford University Prof. Robert Sapolsky (2004).

And nothing brought that basic fact of life home in contemporary America in stunning imagery than the aftermath of Hurricane Katrina. It was beamed out across the globe. Peradventure the spontaneous utterance of CNN correspondent Wolf Blitzer in response to what was evident to everyone looking on; he said "these people are so poor and so black, this is bound to raise questions." He took some heat for that remark, but I fail to see why. If we were completely honest with ourselves, the notion of refugee status came to mind for many. A refugee is someone who is essentially cut off from the social world around them; someone who is displaced, someone who have lost their social bearing and sense of belonging. Yet how could such a population carry on in America and be so maladaptively disconnected from those around them? In other news the Associated Press (AP) did an article on the use of the word "refugee" as descriptive of the people who were victimized by Hurricane Katrina (9/7/2005). Due to the racial sensitivity of those affected, Jesse Jackson and others thought the word carried racist implications. On the other hand others thought that such words as "evacuees" or the "displaced" were too clinical and perhaps could be used as a tool to minimize the dire circumstances of those affected. Sometimes I find it amazing that we as people cannot simply voice what is right in front of us. As for the AP, Executive Editor Kathleen Carroll thought it best to use the word "refugee." She stated, "[s]everal hundred thousand people have been uprooted from their homes and communities and forced to seek refuge in more than 30 different states across America. Until such time as they are able to take up new lives in their new communities or return to their former homes, they will be refugees."

So the answer as to whether Black America can go it alone is a very simple no. They cannot coexist as a population separated from the broader social community in ways which impact quality of life. And to continue to move in a direction which separates them from mainstream society creates a set of social conditions that are Katrina-like across every sector of life.

Furthermore, "if all the world's a stage" and we are merely social actors acting in context to the social world we find ourselves in, then "acting white" is the thing to do, if doing so means matching a set of advantageous life habits to distinctive social challenges to then succeed in society at large. In a cruel irony, the end result of much of what black culture offers its adherents currently got its start in an environment of harsh subjugation where blacks were made to "act black" and in so doing they were made to abide an ignoble social station and moreover wear a smile while doing so. This goes to show just how obsolete, topsy-turvy and disordered this whole social phenomenon has become.

Pastness can be trained on in-group members as well and used to maintain group solidarity (Wallerstein, I. 2000). In fact the notion of "acting white" on the part of blacks has a history which dates back to the era of American slavery. By training that kind of coercion toward an individual who otherwise might feel at ease with the idea of "...taking the responsibility to find the right answer to [his] problems and to fulfill the tasks which it constantly sets for each individual." Should he succumb to the mocking, he takes his place among all those that have ensured their defeat in the world and in life.

Used in this way, to mock such persons is designed to strike at the quick of one's sensitivity to rejection. Belongingness researchers Baumeister and Leary (2000) refer to our evolutionary instilled "sociometer" designed to be keenly aware of detecting threats to our sense of belonging. In other words, we are more aware, more sensitive to detecting decrements than increments in belongingness (Haselton & Buss 2000). This fact of the human condition "operates in an automatic manner (i.e., continuously, involuntarily, and unconsciously)" according to evolutionary psychologists David Buss and Haselton.

One thing is for sure however, no matter whether one is Black or White or anything in between; there are certain unavoidable realities which stem from our universal nature as human beings which are in need of fulfillment. Call it applied evolutionary psychology. One such fact is this: "Something inherent in our biological makeup motivates us to try and improve, or at least maintain, our standing against those with whom we compete for important positional resources" (Frank, R. 1985). And that "mental health results from the fulfillment of archetypal goals" (Steven & Price 2000).

The Black community is mired in pathology associated with issues centered on belongingness. It very well may be that they are not aware of the associations between belongingness, specifically social engagement and the fulfillment of quality of life issues. Otherwise, "...why get in the car and head off in the direction of a place you don't really want to reach?" (Klaus, M. p.13).

What was once a normal reaction to an abnormal situation—the enslavement of a population of people and their cultural orientation as the way to survive in the face of endless struggle—is now an outmoded way of looking at contemporary American society. It is by definition a culture of poverty maintained by the perpetuation of learned helplessness.

However to say "a culture of poverty" for most of us is often misleading. This is due the fact that we tend to think of a financial or economics endowment as the panacea and it's not. I'm inclined to believe, and there is much about the nature of "black poverty" to suggest, that the remedies intersect a host of sociocultural domains. Economist William Easterly (2006) understands the nature of a culture of poverty in this way: "poverty is a complicated tangle of political, social, historical, institutional, and technological factors" (p.6). To remedy such a longstanding state of affairs in the African American community, it must begin by removing the conditions under which such a state is allowed to perpetuate itself.

The central question in all of this is: have we embarked upon a time in civil society where an individual of color can experience full social participation and autonomy? If so, then perhaps the time has come where the tables are in need of being turned; where the one who is "acting white" is more accurately acting normatively and in a manner more consistent with today's challenges as opposed one of a bygone era.

In short, what we are after here is a kind of enlightenment observed by Steven Pinker (2002) when he wrote, "(w)hen conventions are widely enough entrenched, they can become a kind of reality even though they only exist in people minds...they consist in a shared understanding in the minds of most members in a community, usually agreements to grant (or deny) power or status to certain other people...and it can change, dissolve with changes in the collective psychology" (p. 65).

There needs to be a change in the collective psychology for sure. But that will never happen as long as individuals within the black community rely upon the power of past-ness to sway those who are at maximum risk to do nothing individually redeeming in today's social environment.

Perhaps President Obama can help. Speaking at the Democratic National Convention in 2004 (and I imagine speaking Standard English so as to make himself understood) he said:

> "Go into any inner-city neighborhood, and folks will tell you that government alone can't teach kids to learn. They know that parents have to parent, that children can't achieve unless we raise their expectations and turn off the television sets and eradicate the slander that says a black youth with a book is acting white."

****

OBSERVATIONS OF AN OREO

...If we can understand how it is that we participate in the construction of our own realities, then we can take a more active and purposeful approach toward making this the sort of world in which we want to live.

Jodi O'Brien

I imagine to most people when they consider the title of this work and what an "Oreo" means in terms of his or her social identity, personality, sense of self and self-worth, and cultural outlook; it's conceivable to think of that person as someone who is in conflict with themselves. In so far as outwardly—obvious physical features place them firmly within the confines of one race. Yet in seeming contrast to that placement the kind of purchase such persons strive to possess on life departs in significant ways from how their group or collective identity is understood in the general course of life.

It's the result of two divergent life histories and the potent legacies they have spawned. This observation is one of which we here in this nation are keenly aware of because it harkens back to something definitive about American history. It's one of Malcolm Gladwell's "Blink" (2005) moments; "the power of thinking without thinking" in so far as in an instance, it seems the totality of race relations in American history has the ability to sweep through the corridors of our minds. One of the endpoints of this process is the significant ways in which there is something essential about Blacks and Whites and their respective cultural identity that will always stand in stark contrast to each other. It dates back to that binary system of racial categorization, where Blacks epitomized the central paradigm of racial "otherness" (Goldstein, E. L. 2006) not only in terms of obvious physical features such as eye, hair and skin color but also in sociality, intelligence and outlook on the world as well.

In the study of psychology this observation is called entitativity. Back in 1958 a gentleman working in the field of behavioral science coined the phrase to describe how humankind's skilled social functioning make sense of the social world through the impressions we gather from individuals that ties them to groups (Campbell, D.T. 1958). We gather and collate these social experiences and perceptions which in turn are grouped together, saving us from the time and trouble of having to discover the social world around anew each time we encounter it.

Can you imagine upon encountering a deranged individual who is bent on taking your life—from whom you barely escape his clutches only to encounter the same person on a different day? Who would you rather be? The person who remembers the encounter and takes precautionary measures, or the person who has to go about re-establishing a baseline experience with that person? Skilled social functioning precludes us from doing the latter. And more than that, you make note of the characteristics of that person with the intent of being highly avoidant of him and "others" like him. To gather impressions and collate them in this fashion is to group individuals who share some important similarities.

The natural world around us testifies to its adaptiveness. Most have heard of the expression "birds of a feather flock together." This behavior can be seen among various species and among various races of a species of animal. As zoologist Ernst Mayr (2002) writes, "races are not something specifically human; races occur in a large percentage of species of animals." But feathers are only skin deep. Yet in our observations of the natural world the nature of a racial population or the species in question goes beyond mere appearances. They can tell us much about the depth of their group cohesiveness, whom they seem to exclude, and in-group mating practices. They clue us in to social things.

For the purpose of this discussion entitativity helps us to understand the function and importance of a social group. We do this by assessing the degree of similarity like persons exhibit. "Campbell (1958) emphasized three cues that individuals can use to make judgments regarding entitativity: *common fate* (the extent to which individuals in the aggregate seem to experience interrelated outcomes), *similarity* (the extent to which the individuals display the same behaviors or resemble one another), and *proximity* (the distance between individuals in the aggregate)" (Forsyth, D.R. 2010, found in Wiki 2014).

Without groups there can be no sense of belonging. In other words, where the human need to belong is concerned groups, are essential. Be they racial groups with an accumulated culture that answered some important survival questions across that group's history. Or religious groups and their practices with their own prescriptive culture defining who they will and will not accept. Both embed value propositions. In some essential ways human groups and our placement or subscription to them shapes our sense of self by defining who we are in the social world and to whom we belong.

There is also cognitive compatibility where our social identity provides coherence to our feeling of belongingness, our sense of self in terms of shared in-group attributes. There is simpatico, friendship, liking and even the sense of family and a home away from home. It also generates group behaviors such as ethnocentrism, conformity, cohesion, stereotyping, intergroup competition and discrimination. It offers us prototypes by way of socialization that prescribe how we are to see ourselves and others around us through a consensus that says 'we' are like this, and 'they' are like that. In an adaptive sense we derive skilled social functioning making the social world and the behaviors of people more predictable, allowing us to avoid harm, plan effectively, and shaping how we are to feel and behave (Hogg, M.A. 2005).

Throughout all of this, one thing is for sure, it is impossible to know, gauge or experience any of this without history. We arrive at our present only through history. It answers a question once asked, "Why do we need a social past? (Wallerstein, I. 2000). "There is no such thing as an *a*historical person" says Hazel Markus, a cultural psychologist of Stanford University. And indeed history is the central issue where "the Oreo" is concerned, given the explicit representation of two historical opposites rolled into one person. "Race implicates power and indexes the history or ongoing imposition of one group's authority over another. Usually a racial designation signals that differences between groups may be the result of one group maintaining another group as different (and usually inferior)" (Markus, H. 2008).

To step outside of the fishbowl and think more broadly or globally about human history and the nature of human conflict. "Throughout our species' history, intergroup conflict depended on the categorization of the social world into *us* versus *them*. When this divide occurs along racial lines, this categorization and its malignant consequences appear capable of persisting stably" (Kurzban, Tooby & Cosmides 2001).

We learned earlier that before Great Britain became Great Britain, it was simply a region of Europe whose human populations were enslaved by the Romans. And even after the Romans were forced to leave the area, the progress in terms of sociality and technology the Romans had infused into the region and its people fell into disarray as Barbarians sweeping in from places like Germania took possession of it. In doing so they upended the social progress which took place under Roman rule, returning what we now know as the British Isle once again to an intellectual backwater (Sowell, T. 1998).

The point being, what could said about race relations across American history could in fact be said about human group relations and coalitional arms races throughout all time. You may recall the comments on human nature made by evolutionary biologist Richard Alexander on page 13. Ecological dominance and social competition was/is the driving force behind human intelligence (Flinn, M.V. et al. 2005). Also, "once groups of human beings became the main source of competition, a race situation developed where there was no real limit to the degree of intelligence required to master social life, since the other social actors were gaining intelligence at an equal rate" (Fukuyama, F. 1999). That is the human condition, it is something that is very much alive and well among us today and we are all far better off by understanding it than ignoring it.

As for the historical present, while notions of being a colorblind and multicultural society is something this nation earnestly endeavors to approximate. Issues with a polarizing racial angle nonetheless continue to surface from time to time making us Oreos and the nature of our sense of self seem even more dichotomous. It is on those occasions that it takes a social outlook where being more of a citizen of the world is more advantageous than just of Athens.

If it was all just "an act," if it was a mere superficial affectation as stated by those who implore such persons "to keep it real," then it would be something easily abandoned in those times. The fact that such persons continue on in spite of some troubling racial occurrences should suggest depth and value propositions which cannot be so easily abandoned any more than someone can abandon any other aspects of their personality.

Notwithstanding some of the contemplations others may have of us Oreos may in fact be true simply because people are complex as well as the social environment at large. To begin with there is always "the power of the social situation" which at times can be the central issue directing human behavior. We all tend to underestimate the strength of the social context (Milgram, S. & Sabini, J. 1983). I touched on this in the introduction. A main component of social interactions for all people and especially for African Americans are "confirmation biases: the tendency to reach for information that confirms one's preconceptions" (Myers, D.G. 2004). Also there are adaptive self-delusions (Trivers, R. 2011) that motivate all persons toward achieving important life goals, and this is especially true of the Oreo, given that such people are the exceptions and not the rule. There are 'fundamental attribution errors" that have to be navigated where society at large is more apt to attribute a behavior to something essential about being black rather than the power of the social situation.

Where applicability of all that was just mentioned is concerned; consider as well this question once posed: "Is the underclass black? ....So yes, the problem we are talking about is the culture of our largely black (and largely urban) ghettos. It is only part of the problems facing black Americans, although all blacks are unfairly stigmatized by the behavior of the underclass minority" (Kaus, M. 1987 p.106). Sadly, since the time of that comment, 1987, what was then a minority of the black population has become the majority as of 2014. So in truth navigating all of that takes a kind of social intelligence that is in some ways unique to us Oreos. But humans possess the ability to use theory of mind to understand the motivations of those around them, and so they understand the Oreo as well.

Unpacking this to some degree and arguing for the authenticity of such individuals is what this contribution is intended to do. By way of conversation, some time ago, I was working on the manuscript which inspired this piece and attempting to expand my understanding of human behavior (psychology) while working at my job which pays money. A co-worker approached and asked me what was I studying? She had recently moved from Berkeley Ca. where she was involved with the University of Cal Berkeley and was accustomed to seeing similar scenes of individuals buried in books and professional articles. But rather than giving her an answer directly I let her read the first three paragraphs of the manuscript. Germane to this story she is a woman of European ancestry and after reading it, her utterance under her breath was, "wow, being African American has got to be one of the most complex social identities one could have." To which I said, "You're telling me."

Concordantly, the nature of this work is complex and fraught with many potential pitfalls. Here I am arguing that the time has arrived in contemporary society where to hold on to the past and past ways of thinking, behaving and feeling is a very debilitating way of navigating the social world presently. I can say that because it's true.

Furthermore here I am proclaiming this in the face of a set of crucial social events which seemingly possess a steep racial angle, such as the skyrocketing rate of incarceration among black males. This phenomenon does in fact possess a racial angle. But the way in which it's understood is skewed. And this misapprehension is biased in a way which jettisons African Americans back to a time in American history where race relations were in greater opposition. The result is the hurling of blame toward mainstream society at a time when the broader society is trending toward a mindset whereby they refuse to own something like that any longer. This stalemate terminates in inertia that channels the ongoing social isolation.

It's not that America itself is home to an unsympathetic population; far from it as we learned earlier. Most understand how history has followed populations into the present, perpetuating some of the disparate outcomes seen in Black America when compared to America Proper. But my guess is that none of them feel like they are a part of some vast conspiracy to eviscerate the humanity of Black America.

In a departure from all of that, my aim then is consistent with those who seek to better understand a phenomenon in order to subvert the sequence of events that maintains it and perpetuates old modes of social thinking. "Understanding is more often used to try to alter an outcome than to repeat or perpetuate it. That's why psychologists try to understand the minds of murderers and rapists, why social historians try to understand genocide, and why physicians try to understand the causes of human disease. Those investigators do not seek to justify murder, rape, genocide, and illness. Instead, they seek to use their understanding of a chain of causes to interrupt the chain" (Diamond, J. 1999).

At the same time however, there is a formidable element to this discussion that pits me and the argument I'm presenting in almost head-on conflict with those who would rather cleave to "past ways" of thinking, feeling and behaving because to them it best explains what is taking place presently. Simply because to take the time to free oneself from the ghost of those "past ways" is understood as the ultimate betrayal to a set of cultural habits that signals solidarity with those of one's race even as the social environment at large is riddled with reasons why one should not.

Granted, history and the fallout from it can be a monster and a labyrinth to both understand and step out of. And racial designations such as Black and White and the paradigm of distinctive racial otherness they suggest sets up a kind of socio-historical opposition unlike any other. "These are the labels of group-hood which history made sure would eventually be attached to our psychological self as we arrived in the world within the confines of this family rather than that one" (Milton, G. 1964 p.26).

Therefore upon taking me at face value, I'm supposed to be something of a walking contradiction in so far as "the customs of a society are an accumulation of its collective approvals and disapprovals" (Singer, P. 1981 p.94). Culture can be defined as the art of survival. And black culture at least in America is mostly an accumulation of ideas, behaviors and folkways of bearing up under the imposition of subjugation. That past in this case has bred a kind of hardened resolve among the oppressed resulting in a hard-edged and exaggerated social and cultural identity that seeks to be equal to the amount of psychological distance they've experienced over time (Henderson, M.D. 2009). That psychological distance over the last 50 years or so has become a kind of default and social currency that some or perhaps most African Americans would rather hold on to than relinquish.

An "Oreo" in one sense is simply someone who has found a way of liberating themselves from that kind of thinking. But cultural identity is inexorably tied to collective identity. To depart from the bosom of a distinctively black culture with its "exaggerated group identity" makes copying "others"—in this case white culture and its collective identity—akin to treason (Sowell, T. 1994).

Turning our attention to the gene-culture coevolutionary process as a crucial component to this narrative. Biology is a primary factor whereby race is determined. Human behavioral biology works in an autocatalytic fashion with culture to make persons more fit, by way of reproduction, for what they encounter in the world around them. Of these two features, culture is the more plastic: it has the potential to be amenable to change. Renowned biologist E.O. Wilson (1999) says as much when he wrote:

> The nature of the genetic leash and the role of culture can now be better understood, as follows. Certain cultural norms also survive and reproduce better than competing norms, causing culture to evolve in a track in parallel to and usually much faster than genetic evolution. The quicker the pace of cultural evolution, the looser the connection between genes and culture, although the connection is never completely broken. Culture allows a rapid adjustment to changes in the environment through finely tuned adaptations invented and transmitted without corresponding precise genetic prescription (p.139).

Therefore while we may understand that individuals possess the potential to make cultural adjustments or at least we are aware of this attribute; we must also realize that the motivations for doing so, or lack thereof, figures largely into the decision to achieve or avoid a possible outcome. How individuals come upon these important conclusions may not be as straightforward as one would think it'd be. What this suggests is that culture can be as sticky as one's own genetic makeup. This holds even when it is readily understood that culture as the art of survival is operating in a fashion that is in total opposition to survival enhancement. Or so it seems. But how does something like that get started?

"What may start out as rational choice can become cultural artifacts over time" says political scientist Francis Fukuyama (1995) of Stanford University. Fukuyama further explains that culture can and does function as ethical code and in this way culture can also be understood in terms of what it's not. It is not rational choice. "Once it's used to constrain behavior; culture operates more as ethical habit than rational choice. When this is the case [culture] changes very slowly—much more slowly than ideas" (p.40).

Illustrative of this point is an ongoing trend within our society that has emerged over the last few decades. As diversity continues to increase in our nation, integration slows. At its bottom, racial populations in general and especially black America are trending toward neighborhoods which reflect their sense of peoplehood and collective identity. As a result African Americans as a group continue to experience a social segregation that ranks as the nation's highest. Most see this as problematic for Black America given the fact that a founding principle of the civil rights movement of the 60's was social inclusion as opposed to isolation under the old "separate but equal" paradigm.

> Brown University sociologist John Logan is among the first scholars to analyze new U.S. census data on social, economic, housing, and demographic factors for every community in the nation. His findings show that as diversity in the nation grows, progress toward integrating

neighborhoods appears to have stopped. "This is a surprising result," said Logan, director of Brown's Initiative in Spatial Structures in the Social Sciences and director of US2010. "At worst, it was expected that there would be continued slow progress. The growth of the black middle class, the passage of time since fair housing legislation was enacted, and the evidence from surveys that white Americans are becoming more tolerant of black neighbors all pointed in that direction."
(https://news.brown.edu/articles/2010/12/census)

Integration into mainstream society inexorably means participation. It means appropriating a set of cultural attributes or competencies that will allow one to effectively engage society at large and its institutions. There is ruthlessness to this in that to live within the confines of a complex society such as ours and to not engage it is to ensure your defeat. We already see it all around us. Separation occurs, the human need to belong goes unfulfilled and one's sense of belongingness suffers. Social mistrust increases as prosocial behaviors decrease (Twenge, J.M. et al. 2007). The pain of exclusion ensues (William, K.D. 2007) and the cascade continues as low participation in society at large continues, bringing about a crescendo of maladaptive consequences such as a host of diseases with a psychosocial etiology leading to increased mortality (Marmot, M.G. 2006).

Over the last half of the 20th century this nation has seen the emergence of several minority groups go on to become what are understood as "model minorities." In this fashion the notion that one needs to "work their way toward whiteness" is something that is no longer a requirement of success in contemporary society. These are racial groups previously identified by the "color line." Nonetheless, to say that a minority population is a model is to say that, as a group, they embody a high degree of social, economic and academic success. In short they have effectively integrated into mainstream American society—America Proper—in spite of what they look like, or whatever ethnic distinctions that might generally characterize group members.

By contrast the distance which gauges success from failure includes factors such as crime rate, high school dropouts, inter-generational illiteracy, and the subverting of the traditional family structure and stability—all being the seed beds that give rise to social isolation and defeat (Hymowitz, K.S., 2005). Over the course of this time as well whenever a minority population would rise to be considered a model, each time it seemed, their success was to the chagrin of one of America's longest running minority group: African Americans. This holds even after all the help that they've been given. The same help that our young Oreo which began this narrative couldn't bring himself to overlook.

Today the concerns among social science researchers as to why Black America continues to lag behind on important social indexes echoes those of the broader society. The reason being is that strictly in terms of being different, where difference is simply a matter of superficial surface differences; otherness in contemporary America society is commonplace. "For the first time in history, across much of the world, to be foreign is a perfectly normal condition. It is no more distinctive than being tall, fat, or left handed. Nobody raises an eyebrow at a Frenchman in Berlin, a Zimbabwean in London, a Russian in Paris, a Chinese in New York" (*The Economist,* 12/19/2009/2010).

With human diversity being true of the world in general how much more is it true for a nation of immigrants. Ours is a progressive society employing abstract principles to an eclectic mix of people with multi-variant social, religious and political positions and subjective points of view. With such a rich diversity of people within a specific geographic area, if a particular group of individuals is making themselves visible through the replication of a set of behaviors with either good or bad, positive or negative outcomes; chances are they themselves are playing an important role in that phenomenon. Distinctive behavioral traits and attitudes can be (and are) considered "behavioral identity badge(s)" (Pinker, S. 2002 p.66).

Moreover, as a kind of way of looking at the disconnect between mainstream society and many African Americans who cleave to their role as history's victims; social science researchers continue to try and provide answers that explain the current social conditions whose trends are ill-fated. They operationalize this investigation thusly: "this work is a critical means of answering the important question of why, given the minimization of structural barriers to equality, members of traditional stigmatized groups continue to experience relatively poorer health, lower achievement outcomes, and greater psychological alienation than members of non-stigmatized groups" (Downey, G. et al. 2005 p. 45).

To be sure no social disconnect and psychological alienation from civil society is greater than the mark of a convict. This is especially true for Blacks because it has come to be such a trademark and identity badge of the black male. As of March 2006, more than 8 years ago, an article published in the New York Times discusses the conclusions of a joint study performed by three of the nation's top universities. They noted that "a huge pool of poorly educated black men are becoming ever more disconnected from mainstream society... finishing high school is the exception... and prison is almost routine with incarceration rates climbing for blacks even as urban crime rates have declined." In another article entitled "It's Hard Out Here for a Black Man!" in that same year, a writer of African American descent begins the article with this byline: "a welter of statistics, a veritable misery index of facts, suggest that black American men are on the brink of extinction" (Boyd, H. 2006).

That's the nature of "Black failure" and it is a phenomenon that is more than 50 years in the making and the trend is unmistakable. With the advent of ever increasing levels of personal freedom as a result of social progress in contemporary society, individuals are free to pursue one's goals absent the kind of social oppression experienced in times past. Yet in a miscarriage of everything the civil rights movement stood for; this in turn has had the unintended effect of creating an atmosphere which allows for the expansion of a set of debilitating behaviors as opposed to a shrinkage.

Prior to 2006 a number of books aimed at addressing this distressing event and providing guidance to this population have seen publication. In 1997 a joint effort on the part of two African American luminaries, Cornel West and Dr. Henry Louis Gates, issued a work entitled: *The Future of the Race.*" The central idea of the book seeks to recapture an in-group strategy where those that can do, help those that find the going difficult. These two scholars make use of an essay written more than 100 years ago by W.E.D Du Bois and his notion of "the talented tenth." As Du Bois saw it, the talent pool of this population, estimated at ten percent was to advance efforts to uplift those who were struggling socially and economically. This in turn would begin a sea change among a population of people who were much in need of something socially positive and redeeming.

But cultural change is hard to affect. And it's proven to be just as hard for those who presumably are working within the confines of the culture itself as oppose to outsiders who may not have the wherewithal to genuinely connect culturally with this population. Another black luminary is Tavis Smiley. He has published a number of books which concern themselves with the plight of Black America and the increasing black underclass. He too, by word and by deed is someone who is leading by example and putting words into action. The central theme of his work is synonymous with that of Dr. Gates & Cornell West. Yet in spite of the best of their combined efforts; the trend they sought to quell continues on unabated and on some social indexes the trend has increased in ways that are perplexing.

For instance a more recent publication *"The New Jim Crow: mass incarceration in the age of colorblindness"* by Michele Alexander (2010) documents a rate of incarceration among African American males that continues to astound.

But in my estimation and I imagine in the estimation of most people, nothing should invoke a greater sense of urgency as when one sees their own children being swallowed up by the same ogre that has just about engulfed the entire male population of a race of people. Children are just that—they are children in the process of developing; growing both physically and psychologically. To introduce something so socially and psychologically stunting as an arrest by police so early in a child's life simply has to be something that will influence that individual for a lifetime.

Where human belongingness is concerned and the idea that we are all interconnected through cause and effect as Melville opined, without question the entirety of society loses when this is jeopardized, no matter what the racial background of the child being arrested actually is. As a society, when we are able to document a trend of this kind something significant needs to take place to avert the eventual fallout of allowing this to continue unabated.

This latest phenomenon that is sweeping through Black America is something that is nationwide in scope and has been deemed "the school to prison pipeline." A host of online news outlets have covered the story. In a piece done by NPR writer Gene Demby (March 21, 2014) entitled *"Black Preschoolers More Likely To Be Suspended"* it features Education Secretary Arne Duncan and Attorney General Eric Holder and their joint attempt to examine these outcomes with an eye toward ensuring that racial bias is not at the heart of the matter.

At issue is the notion that disciplinary action is meted out too harshly when African American students are involved leading to an arrest as opposed to a visit to the principal's office for disciplinary action. The hope is that with a change in policy where disciplinary action is handled "in-house," as opposed to involving the police, this will solve the ongoing phenomenon of children of color having to undergo arrest and the defeated life path that that experience comes encumbered with. Who doesn't want that! For sure, society as a whole would only benefit from the success of such a plan of action. To gain greater insight into this issue I suggest you visit the NPR website as the featured piece embeds links that allows for greater exploration (http://tiny.cc/cbbdqx).

On another level and perhaps the greater lesson to be learned in all of this can be taken from an example in the not too distant past. If the cultural edict in Black America is to remember where one came from, then for once let a positive example shine through rather than remembrances of failure. "The Little Rock Nine" as they are called is one such example. These were the kids of color that were marshaled into school by armed guards in Little Rock, Arkansas in 1957.

Should one take the time to review a documentary of that turbulent time in American history, one cannot help but find oneself humbled by the sheer poise and strength of character these kids exhibited as hell was breaking loose all around them. Heart palpitating hatred was at a fever pitch as they approached the school campus and the onlookers minced no words as to how they felt about them. Commenting on the steadfastness of the "Little Rock Nine" Oprah Winfrey said this:

> I thank God that I was not born in that time and would not have to be tested in that way. I don't know if I could have stood that test. So I can't even IMAGINE... where you find the strength within yourself to get up... putting on your clothes, shoes, doing your hair and knowing that you're going into an environment where all day long people not only want to spit on you... but do!

If the Civil Rights Movement was an act of civil disobedience which brought attention to social injustice then the Little Rock Nine was a clinic on how to maintain civility and poise (a behavioral identity badge) in a frightening and hostile environment unlike any experienced by the children of today. The lesson today's kids can learn from the Little Rock Nine is simply, the Little Rock Nine couldn't afford to have behavioral problems. And with a litany of failed social programs designed to bring African American kids up to par with their contemporaries spanning the last four decades; neither do today's black youth.

The children who survived that turbulent time in history wanted earnestly to partake of an America that was better than the one they came out of: "separate but equal." Ironically, with the maintenance of a cultural outlook better suited for the actual era of Jim Crow, today's kids all too often are recapitulating something their ancestors fought hard to lay waste to. The "Little Rock Nine" required police escorts into school whereby they could lay hold of their fate making it better. Today's black youth can't even find it within themselves to simply behave well enough to try and learn something. As a result significant numbers of black preschoolers nationwide are being escorted out of school under police arrest thus sealing their fate.

****

Many books and articles which proclaim that colorblindness is really just a new way of rationalizing and justifying racial inequality have come to the fore in recent years. Many of them are well meaning. Generally speaking, many people in public life may have a mistaken impression of what a colorblind society actually is in practical terms independent of magical thinking. For sure it isn't the idea that we should all go around pretending that we don't encode race. A number of studies have confirmed, mostly from the field of social neuroscience, "that people encode the race of each individual they encounter, and do so via computational processes that appear to be both automatic and mandatory" (Kurzban, R. et al. 2001). In certain instances we are keenly aware of race as a component of some social phenomena. An everyday example of this would be the disproportionate number of African Americans in track and field, basketball or football. In very simple terms that is either true or it isn't. In addition, I would hope that the section on how we make sense of the social world around us did something to help our understanding in this regard. Because in like manner, just like all those sports listed above; they all assume human competition. But so do all other activities where one can gain economic resources and status. And for better or for worse, many of the longstanding safeguards which sought to ensure blacks a place at the table are in the process of sundowning. So ready or not it is happening.

If you are a white person, sometimes you can't win with this colorblind thing. That's the twist of an article entitled: *"Seeing Race and Seeming Racist? Whites Go Out of Their Way to Avoid Talking About Race"* (APA Online Oct. 6, 2008). It opens this way, "White people—including children as young as 10—may avoid talking about race so as not to appear prejudiced, according to new research. But that approach often backfires as blacks tend to view this "colorblind" approach as evidence of prejudice, especially when race is clearly relevant." In the case of Wolf Blitzer and the coverage of the Hurricane Katrina aftermath; he clearly saw race and said as much. That landed him in a bit of trouble. That makes it hard to know what to do the next time something like that arises.

Nevertheless, researcher Evan Apfelbaum (2008) at Tufts University says: "Efforts to talk about race are fraught with the potential for misunderstandings... one way that whites try to appear unbiased is to avoid talking about race altogether, a tendency we refer to as strategic colorblindness."

Perhaps the better way to go is to simply become invisible. Surprisingly there is an "invisible model minority" among us. They are the recent immigrants from the continent of Africa. Emerging research regarding this immigrant population indicates that recent African immigrant attainments in education are comparable to those of Asian populations (http://www.jstor.org/stable/i350389). Also the progeny of this population overwhelmingly tend to continue on the path of upwardly social progress begun by their parents (http://tiny.cc/2obdqx).

In an article done by The New York Times more than a decade ago entitled: *"Top Colleges Take More Blacks, But Which Ones?"* The article proceeds to identify "which ones?" by revealing the demographics of those black students as mostly the children of recent African immigrants, West Indian and mixed-race children (http://tiny.cc/otbdqx).

For America's invisible model minority this key is a mindset toward social integration as indicated below.

Black African immigrants generally fare well on integration indicators. Overall they are well educated with college completion rates that greatly exceed those for most other immigrant groups and U.S. natives. In fact, the United States, Canada and Australia disproportionately attract better educated African migrants, while those who are less educated tend to go to the United Kingdom, France and other European countries. Black Africans immigrants in the United States have relatively high employment rates (exceeding 70 percent for most countries of origin). Black African women are also substantially more likely to work than women from other immigrant groups; the exceptions are women from Muslim countries such as Egypt, Morocco, Somalia and Sudan. (http://tiny.cc/2w8wtx)

By contrast, Ta-Nehisi Coates reported on an abysmal state of being and forecast for native-born African Americans as he made his case for reparations. He wrote, "Chicago's black neighborhoods—characterized by high unemployment and households headed by single parents—are not simply poor; they are 'ecologically' distinct." And where the children of native-born African Americans are concerned he said, "the implications are chilling. As a rule, poor black people do not work their way out of the ghetto—and those who do often face the horror of watching their children and grandchildren tumble back." It seems to be the tale of two populations. Both are people of color. The one as we just read possesses the ability to engage society at large resulting in positive outcomes. The other, as it was told us, hovers near the brink of extinction, socially disconnected and isolated and in need of reparations to restore them.

Those who live outside of that fishbowl don't see reparations as the answer. The reason being a wide array of reparations has already run its course in the form of government subsidized programs. President Johnson's "The Great Society," for example, which "was meant to facilitate the entry of minorities into the open society of opportunity and self-fulfillment, but all too often drew them into a closed society of chronic dependency" (Himmelfarb, G. 1999). "A closed society" existing inside an open one has the potential of becoming "ecologically distinct" over time both in biology and in culture.

No one seems to know what the remedy truly is. For Ta-Nehisi Coates something as simple as suggesting that African American males can help themselves by pulling their pants up over their rear ends is perceived as putting them down. I'm sorry, but when you have grown men who do not possess a basic sense of decorum to know that in polite society one should pull their pants up over their rear ends, that speaks volumes about that person to onlookers. Nothing says I'm "black" quite like that. Yet to acknowledge what that person is blatantly transmitting, about his sense of self, is somehow wrong.

A theory first heard in 1987 seems only more salient now given the fact that in 1987 the black underclass had gone from consisting of a minority of the black population to that of the majority. According to Alan Bloom an American philosopher in his contribution *"The Closing of the American Mind"* (1987), the failed attempt to create a significant black presence in American universities during the Affirmative Action years taught us the lesson that "black students have proven "indigestible." They do not "melt as have all other groups." The problem, he contends, "is that blacks have become black... they have become ethnic."

****

THE FUTURE OF AN ALBATROSS

They act freely, but their freedom is constrained by their biographies and the social prisons of which they are a part. Analyzing their biographies and the social prisons liberates them to the maximum degree that they can be liberated. To the extent that we each analyze our social prisons, we liberate ourselves from their constraints to the extent that we can be liberated.

Immanuel Wallerstein

It's hard to know exactly how to conclude something like this narrative. At the start of this writing, I had in mind that I would only go to about 10,000 words in length. At the conclusion of this piece I am more than 30,000 words into it. The threshold question this piece has sought to explore, the thesis if you will, is the same one all other racial (to include white people) and ethnic groups have had to ask themselves either explicitly or tacitly across the generations. "Could one be American and yet retain cultural, ethnic and linguistic differences without becoming a second-class citizen" (de la Campa, Roman, intro to "Magical Urbanism" 2000 by Mike Davis)? And that is indeed the urgent question at hand for many in Black America going forward.

One way to conclude this narrative would be to imagine that I was a father to a child whose heritage has the potential to place him at maximum risk in a social environment where he would need to compete on equal terms with all others of his generation from various historical trajectories; that is, individuals from various racial populations. That seems to make the most sense to me.

I would start by telling him that the warning signs are all around him. That due to a set of historical facts he may find that the racial population to which most will assign him to, and indeed he also may assign himself to due to the fact that race is not a meaningless concept, are in the midst of being relegated to a form of social, economic and intellectual isolation that will be Katrina-like in its appearance. A sociologically evolving twist on what John Kenneth Galbraith (1958, 2002) called "insular poverty" were "forces, common to all members of the community... [which] restrain or prevent participation in economic life at the going rates of returns" which in turn perpetuates the "social prisons" of which Wallerstein spoke. And that he should avoid that fate at all cost.

Furthermore, I would tell him that there is a social world out there that is always in a state of flux. Currently, the people of the world, and indeed the people of our modern society are in the process of caring less and less about what he or anyone else actually looks like in terms of racial makeup. The only thing that truly matters is whether or not he is willing to engage society to the degree all others do and that he can perform the tasks set before them. Moreover that the irony he will find is that it will be others who look just like him that will care far more than most others as to what he is in terms of racial heritage.

I would tell him that people have a need to belong and be approved of no matter how "free" an individual may think he is of such things. I would tell him that as in all things that concerns human beings, there is always complexity and perhaps that is why social science research in the field of group pride has discovered that people compensate for uncertainty in one domain by seeking out or defaulting to another where belongingness seems more assured.

They have found that "(u)ncertainty reduction theory focuses on group identification... as a response to self-uncertainty, and thus it predicts that factors related to group membership, such as inclusion, categorization and entitativity, will influence how strongly people identify with a group as a response to self-uncertainty" says Michael Hogg (2004) of Claremont Graduate University. Furthermore the team of researchers of whom he was a part says that "we can speculate that chronic and extreme levels of uncertainty, perhaps associated with personal or widespread life or societal crises, may motivate people to identify strongly as 'true believers' (Hoffer, 1951) with highly entitative groups—a process where people become entrepreneurs of entitativity, working diligently to perceptually, rhetorically, and actually increase their groups entitativity." In other words: "they have become ethnic." And furthermore: "In extreme cases such groups may have orthodox and ideological beliefs systems, have powerful leaders and zealous, followers [and] be harsh on marginal members and dissidents..." (Baron, Crawley, & Paulina 2003).

****

The word albatross can be used metaphorically to indicate a psychological burden. Other definitions include "something burdensome that impedes action or progress," "an obstacle to success" (free dictionary.com). For the majority of African Americans it seems that the hardest thing to do is to reconsider some aspects of their culture that are producing and reproducing the kinds of results that were highlighted in this discussion.

As a student of human behavior I have heard of a number of discussions of what makes us human and as a result, separate us from all other animals on the planet. Such defining features include "we eat with cutlery" "we cook our food" which allows us consume more calories to feed our enormous brains. The use of fire as a technology with which we cook our food and socialize thus paving the way for us to evolve higher levels of sociality. And probably the most researched would be the ability to use language and with it abstraction and the ability to project ourselves into the future.

Language goes hand in hand with the ability to use reason. Problem solving, being aware of one's own thoughts and possessing the ability to affect one's fate by being able to choose better due to investigation and enlightenment of one's own life. I guess that is why I love the insight given earlier by C. Wright Mills. Recall, he said "... the idea that the individual can understand his own experience and gauge his own fate only by locating himself within his period, that he can know his own life chances only by becoming aware of all those individuals in his circumstances" (p.5). To be African American at this junction in human history and to set one's energies toward manifesting that as both a current and "future self," is to be considered an Oreo.

Sociologically, it is as George Herbert Mead's classic text, Mind Self and Society, established: social identities are created through our ongoing social interaction with other people and our subsequent self-reflection about who we think we are according to these social exchanges. Mead's work shows that identities are produced through agreement, disagreement, and negotiation with other people. We adjust our behaviour and our self-image based upon our interactions and our self-reflection about these interactions (this is also known as the looking glass self; also see http://tiny.cc/14e9sx).

My highest hope for this imaginary son of mine would be that I married intellectually well and that he subsequently inherited his mom's brains. Short of that, I would want him to know that despite what the rest of human society chooses to believe about themselves in terms of the meaninglessness of race, currently, nothing could be further from the truth because culture has biology. In fact, he need only take a moment out to sociologically "locate himself within his period" and he will soon discover that not only is the biology of race and the staying power of culture ruthlessly real but due to the fate of human societies over the last 10,000 years, his heritage has been and continues to be a pedigree of pain. And yes indeed "in many ways... that is a terrible lesson."

Nonetheless, given today's level of personal freedom, even individuals with his heritage can experience a life lived to the fullest. That is something that was categorically impossible for someone with his heritage in times pervious to this one. Today, the potential is there to actualize something that was only accessible to individuals with a pedigree of privilege. In like manner, he could identify with the words written by a great biologist named Rene Dubos (1968) in his book "So Human an Animal." He wrote:

> "The problems I have met while integrating my French heritage with the rich experience of my American life have given me the conviction that each one of us can consciously create his personality and contribute to the future, by using what the world of the present offers him to convert his hereditary and experiential past into a living reality. Scientific knowledge of the effects that surroundings, events, and ways of life exert on human development would give larger scope to human freedom by providing a rational basis for option and action. Man makes himself through enlightened choices that enhance his humanness" (p.xii).

WORKS CITED

Introduction

http://tiny.cc/u6oytx

Marmot, M. (2004). *The status syndrome: how social standing affects health and longevity.* New York, NY: Henry Holt & Co.

Cooley, C.H. (1983). Looking-glass self. In *Human nature and the social order* (pp.182-185). New York: Transaction Publishers. Also, Goffman, E. 1959 *The presentation of self in everyday life.* Garden City N.Y: Doubleday (Taken from: *The Production of Reality 4*th *edition,* (p.255) O'Brien, Jodi. 2006, Thousand Oaks CA: Pine Forge Press.)

Kaus, M. (1995). *The end of equality.* New York, NY: Basic Books.

http://tiny.cc/hl5ytx

Zimbardo, P.E. (1972) Pathology of imprisonment. *Society,* vol. 9, No. 6.

Pinker, S. (1997). *How the mind works.* 1997. New York, NY: Norton.

Harris, L. T., & Fiske, S. T. (2007). Social groups that elicit disgust are differentially processed in mPFC. *Social cognitive and affective neuroscience,* 2(1), 45-51.

Singer, P. (2000). A Darwinian Left: Politics, evolution, and cooperation. New Haven, CT: Yale University Press.

The Newness of an Old Perspective

Wallerstein, I. (2004). *World systems analysis.* Durham, SC: Duke University Press.

Shields, S.A. & Sunil B. (2009) Darwin on race, gender, and culture. *American Psychologist,* vol. 64, no. 2.

The Central Observation

Sowell, T. (1994) *Race and culture* New York, NY: Basic Books.

Lynch, J.W., Kaplan, G.A., & Salonen, J.T. (1997) *Social Science Medicine,* vol. 44., No. 6, pp.809-819.

Moynihan, D. *The Negro family: The case for national action.* United States Department of Labor. Retrieved 22 March. 2014.

Hymowitz, K.S. (2005). *The black family: 40 years of lies.* 2005 (http://tiny.cc/sm5ytx).

Myers, D.G. (2004). *Exploring social psychology (3rd edition).* New York, NY: McGraw-Hill.

Richerson, P.J., Boyd, R., & Henrich, J. (2010). Gene-culture coevolution in the age of genomics. *PNAS,* vol. 107, suppl. 2, pp.8995-8992.

Sokol, R.I., & Stroud, S.L. (2007). Understanding human psychology: the integration of social, evolutionary, and cultural studies. *The Journal of Social, Evolutionary, and Cultural Psychology.* 1(1): pp.1-6.

Cacioppo, J.T. (2000). Autonomic, neuroendocrine, and immune responses to psychological stress. *Psychologische Beitrage, Band 42,* S. 4-23

Cacioppo, J.T., Berntson, G.G., Sheridan, J.F., & McClintock, M.K. (2002). *Psychological Bulletin* November 2000, vol.126, no.6, 829-843.

Darwin, C (2004) *The origin of species.* New York, NY: Barnes & Noble.

Buss, D.M (1999). *Evolutionary psychology: The new science of the mind.* Needham Heights, MA, US: Allyn & Bacon. (1999). xxii 456 pp.

Rowe, D.C. (2005).Under the skin: on the impartial treatment of genetic and environmental hypothesis of racial differences. *American Psychologist.*

Brown, G.R., Dickins, T.E., Sear, R., & Laland, K.N. (2011). Evolutionary accounts of human behavioural diversity. *Philosophical Transactions of the Royal Society B: Biological Sciences, 366* (1563), 313-324.

Balaresque, P. L., Ballereau,S.J., & Jobling, M.A. (2007). Challenges in human genetic diversity: demographic history and adaptation. *Human Molecular Genetics,* vol. 16, review issue 2.

Marmot, M. (2004) *The status syndrome: how social standing affects health and longevity.* New York, NY: Henry Holt & Co.

Risch, N., Burchard, E., Ziv, E., & Tang, H. (2002). Categorization of humans in biomedical research: genes, race, and disease. (http://tiny.cc/3n5ytx).

Diamond, J.M. (1997). *Guns, germs and steel: a short history of everybody for the last 13,000 years.* London: Random House.

Symons, D. (1992). On the use and misuse of Darwinism in the study of human behavior. In Barkow, J.H., Cosmides, L., Tooby, J. *The Adapted Mind.* (pp. 137-159). New York, NY: Oxford University Press.

Richerson, P.J., Boyd, R., & Henrich, J. (2010). Gene-culture coevolution in the age of genomics. *PNAS,* vol. 107, suppl. 2, pp.8995-8992.

The Need to Belong

O'Brien, Jodi. (2006). *The Production of reality (4th edition).* Thousand Oaks, CA: Pine Forge Press.

Rushton, P.J. (1999). Race, evolution & behavior. Brunswick, NJ: Transaction Publishers.

Belongingness: A Basic Human Motivation

http://tiny.cc/505ytx

Singer, P. (2000). A Darwinian Left: politics, evolution, and cooperation. New Haven, CT: Yale University Press.

Markus, H.R. (2008). Pride, prejudice, and ambivalence: toward a unified theory of race and ethnicity. *American Psychologist,* vol. 63, no. 8.

Kaus, M. (1995). *The end of equality.* New York, NY: Basic Books.

Cacioppo, J.T., & Hawkley, L.C. (2009). Perceived social isolation and cognition. *Trends in Cognitive Sciences,* 13, pp. 447-454.

Leary, M.R. (1990). Responses to social exclusion: Social anxiety, jealousy, loneliness, depression, and low self-esteem. *Journal of Social and Clinical Psychology*, vol.9, pp. 221-229.

Morrison, M., Epstude, K., & Roese, N.J. (2012). Life regret and the need to belong. *Social Psychological and Personality Science,* 3, 675.

Baumeister, R.F., & Leary, M.R. (1995). Desire for interpersonal attachment as a fundamental human motivation. *Psychological Bulletin*, vol. 117, pp. 497-529.

Fukuyama, F. (1999). *The Great disruption: Human nature and the reconstitution of social order.* New York, NY: Simon & Schuster.

Pinker, S. (2002). *The blank slate.* New York, NY: Penguin Books.

Baumeister, R.F., & Leary, M.R. (1995). Desire for interpersonal attachment as a fundamental human motivation. *Psychological Bulletin*, vol. 117, pp.497-529.

William, K.D. (2011). The pain of exclusion. *Scientific American.* January/February 2011.

Fukuyama, F. (1995). *Trust: the social virtues and the creation of prosperity.* New York, NY: Simon & Schuster.

Baumeister, R.F., & Leary, M.R. (1995). Desire for interpersonal attachment as a fundamental human motivation. *Psychological Bulletin*, vol. 117 pp.497-529.

West, C. (2001). *Cornel West: a critical reader*. Malden, MA: Blackwell Publishers, Inc.

Bain, P.G., & Kashima, Y.H. (2006). Conceptual beliefs about human values and their implications human nature beliefs predict value importance, value trade-offs, and responses to value-laden rhetoric. *Journal of Personality and Social Psychology,* vol. 91, no.2, pp. 351-367.

Markus, H., & Nurius, P. (1986). Possible selves. *American Psychologist, 41,* 954-959.

Markus, H., & Nurius, P. (1987). Possible selves: The interface between motivation and the self concept. In K. Yardley & T. Honess (Eds.), *Self and identity* (pp. 157-172). Chichester, England: Wiley.

Baumeister, R.F., & Leary, M.R. (1995). Desire for interpersonal attachment as a fundamental human motivation. *Psychological Bulletin*, vol. 117 pp.497-529.

Mills, C.W. (1959). *The sociological imagination*. New York, NY: Oxford University Press.

Melville, H. (1851). Moby Dick. New York, NY: Harper and Brothers.

Baumeister, R.F., & Leary, M.R. (1995). Desire for interpersonal attachment as a fundamental human motivation. *Psychological Bulletin*, vol. 117 pp.497-529.

Wilkinson, G.R. (2000). *Mind the gap: hierarchies, health and human evolution*. New Haven, CT: Yale University Press.

http://tiny.cc/7p5ytx

Baumeister, R.F., & Leary, M.R. (1995). Desire for interpersonal attachment as a fundamental human motivation. *Psychological Bulletin*, vol. 117, pp.497-529.

Coates, T.-N. (June 2014). 250 years of slavery. 90 years of Jim Crow. 60 years of separate but equal. 35 years of state-sanctioned redlining. Until we reckon with the compounding moral debts of our ancestors, America will never be whole. *The Atlantic*.

http://tiny.cc/4q5ytx

http://tiny.cc/3r5ytx

A World of Knowledge

Sutter, M., & Kawecki, T.J. (2009). Influence of learning on range expansion and adaptation to novel habitats. *Journal of Evolutionary Biology,* vol. 22, pp. 2201-2214.

Feldman, R.S. (2003). *Development across the life span.* New Jersey: Prentice Hall.

Mayr, E. (1982). *The growth of biological thought: Diversity, evolution and inheritance.* Cambridge, MA: Harvard University Press.

Cohen, P. (Sept. 2006). Introduction: Genetics. *New Scientist.*

Wilson, E.O. (1998). *Consilience: the unity of knowledge.* New York, NY: Vintage Books.

Henrich, J. (Nov.2011). A cultural species: how culture drove human evolution. *American Psychological Association.*

Queller, D.G. (downloaded on March 3, 2011@ oxfordjournals.org). W.D. Hamilton and the evolution of sociality. *Behavioral Ecology,* vol.12, no. 2, pp. 261-268.

Marks, J. (2010). Ten facts about human evolution. *Human Evolutionary Biology.* Boston, MA: Cambridge University Press.

Amodio, D.M., & Firth, C.D. (2006). Nature reviews. *Neuroscience,* vol. 7, pp. 268-277.

Mayr, E. (1982). *The growth of biological thought: Diversity, evolution and inheritance.* Cambridge, MA. The Belknap Press of Harvard University Press.

Singer, P. (2000). A Darwinian Left: politics, evolution, and cooperation. New Haven, CT: Yale University Press.

Sokol, R.I., & Stroud, S. L. (2007). Understanding human psychology: the integration of social, evolutionary, and cultural studies. *The Journal of Social, Evolutionary, and Cultural Psychology,* 1(1): pp.1-6.

Wilson, E.O. (1998). *Consilience: the unity of knowledge.* New York, NY: Vintage Books.

Mills, C.W. (1959). *The sociological imagination.* New York, NY: Oxford University Press.

The Making of the Modern World

Ferguson, N. (2002). *Empire: How Britain made the modern world.* London: Penguin Books.

http://tiny.cc/0s5ytx

Sowell, T. (1998). *Conquest and cultures.* New York, NY: Basic Books.

Diamond, J. (1999). *Guns, germs and steel.* New York, NY: W.W. Norton.

Fukuyama, F. (1995). *Trust: the social virtues and the creation of prosperity.* New York, NY: Simon & Schuster.

Weber, M. (1930, 1992).*The Protestant ethic and the spirit of capitalism.* London: Routledge.

Spradely, J.P. & McCurdy, D.W. (1987). *Conflict and conformity: Readings in cultural anthropology.* Boston, MA: Little Brown and Co.

Swindler, A. (Apr. 1986). Culture in action: symbols and strategies. *American Sociological Review,* vol. 51, issue 2, pp. 273-286.

How Whiteness Came To Be

Sarich, V., & Miele, F. (2004). *Race: the reality of human differences*. Boulder, CO: Westview Press.

Rowe, D.C. (2005).Under the skin: on the impartial treatment of genetic and environmental hypothesis of racial differences. *American Psychologist*.

Cochran, G., & Harpending, H. (2010). *The 10,000 year explosion: How civilization accelerated human evolution*. New York, NY: Basic Books.

Herrnstein, R.J., & Murray, C. (1994). *The bell curve*. New York, NY: Free Press Paperbacks.

Cochran, G., & Harpending, H. (2010). *The 10,000 Year Explosion: How civilization accelerated human evolution*. New York: Basic Books.

Ward, P. (March 2013). What may become of homo sapiens. *Scientific American*.

Diamond, J. (1999).*Guns, germs and steel*. New York, NY: W.W. Norton

Singer, P. (2000). *A Darwinian Left: politics, evolution, and cooperation*. New Haven, CT: Yale University Press.

Wallerstein, I. (2004). *World systems analysis*. Durham, SC: Duke University Press.

Andrea, A.J., & Overfield, J.H. (1998). *The human record*. Boston, MA: Houghton Mifflin Company.

Fukuyama, F. (1995). *Trust: The social virtues and the creation of prosperity*. New York, NY: Simon & Schuster.

Fukuyama, F. (1999). *The great disruption: Human nature and the reconstitution of social order*. New York, NY: Simon & Schuster.

Searle, J.R. (1995). *The construction of social reality*. New York, NY: The Free Press.

Diamond, J. (1999).*Guns, germs and steel*. New York, NY: W.W. Norton

Working toward Whiteness

Diamond, J. (1999).*Guns, germs and steel*. New York, NY: W.W. Norton

http://tiny.cc/vt5ytx

Milton, G. M. (1964). *Assimilation in American life: The role of race, religion and national origins*. New York, NY: Oxford University Press.

http://tiny.cc/qjdxtx

Markus, H.R. (2008). Pride, prejudice, and ambivalence: toward a unified theory of race and ethnicity. *American Psychologist*, vol. 63, no. 8.

Fiske, S. (2010). Envy up, scorn down: How comparisons divide us. *American Psychologist,* vol.65, no. 8.

Roediger. D.R. (2005). *Working toward whiteness: How America's immigrants became white*. New York, NY: Basic Books.

Dostoyevsky, F. (1993). *Notes from the underground*. New York, NY: Vintage Books

Racial In-Betweeness

Takaki, R (1993). *A different mirror: A historical of multicultural America*. Boston, MA: Little Brown & Co.

Markus, H.R. (2008). Pride, prejudice, and ambivalence: toward a unified theory of race and ethnicity. *American Psychologist,* vol. 63, no. 8.

Darwin, C. (1871). *The descent of man and selection in relation to sex*. London: J Murray.

West, C. (2001). *Cornel West: a critical reader*. Malden, MA: Blackwell Publishers Inc.

Balaresque, P. L., Ballereau, S.J., & Jobling, M.A. (2007). Challenges in human genetic diversity: demographic history and adaptation. *Human Molecular Genetics,* vol. 16, review issue 2.

Rowe, D.C. (2005).Under the skin: on the impartial treatment of genetic and environmental hypothesis of racial differences. *American Psychologist.*

Stix, G. (March 1 2013). Traces of a distant past. *Scientific American.*

Dawkins, R. (2006). *The selfish gene.* Oxford, England: Oxford University Press.

Johnson, A.G. (2001). *Privilege, power, and difference.* Boston, MA: McGraw-Hill.

Gordon, M. (1964). *Assimilation in American life.* Oxford, England: Oxford University Press.

Race in Binary Terms

Goldstein, E.L. (2008). *The Price of whiteness: Jews, race, and American identity.* New Jersey: Princeton University Press.

Balaresque, P. L., Ballereau,S.J., & Jobling, M.A. (2007). Challenges in human genetic diversity: demographic history and adaptation. *Human Molecular Genetics,* vol. 16, review issue 2.

Graham, R. (2002). *Putting psychology in its place: a critical historical overview.* New York, NY: Taylor & Francis.

Diamond, J. (1999).*Guns, germs and steel.* New York, NY: W.W. Norton

Patterson, O. (1982). *Social death.* Boston, MA: Harvard University Press.

Dawkins, R. (2006). *The selfish gene.* Oxford, England: Oxford University Press.

Singer, P. (2000). *A Darwinian Left: politics, evolution, and cooperation.* New Haven, CT: Yale University Press.

Barkow, J.H. (2002). Biology is destiny only if we ignore it. *World Futures*, 2003, vol. 59, pp. 173-188.

Singer, P. (1999). *The expanding circle: ethics and sociobiology*. New York, NY: Farrar, Straus & Giroux.

Baumeister, R.F., & Leary, M.R. (1995). Desire for interpersonal attachment as a fundamental human motivation. *Psychological Bulletin*, vol. 117, pp.497-529.

Acting White

Hogg, M.A., Sherman, D.K., Diereselhuis, J., Maitner, A.T., & Moffitt, G. (2005). Uncertainty, entitativity, and group identification (2005). *Journal of Experiential Social Psychology*.

Frankl, V. (2006). *Man's search for meaning*. Boston, MA: Beacon Press.

Vaughan, D. (1986). *Uncoupling*. New York, NY: Oxford University Press.

Baumeister, R.F., & Leary, M.R. (1995). Desire for interpersonal attachment as a fundamental human motivation. *Psychological Bulletin*, vol. 117, pp.497-529.

Frankl, V. (2006). *Man's search for meaning*. Boston, MA: Beacon Press.

Bonham, V.L., Warschauer-Baker, E., & Collins, F.S. (Jan. 2005). Race and ethnicity in the genome era. *American Psychologist*.

Wang, O.V., & Sue, S. (2005). In the eye of the storm: race and genomics in research and practice. *American Psychologist*.

Wallerstein, I. (2004). *World systems analysis*. Durham, SC: Duke University Press.

Marmot, M. (2004) *The status syndrome: how social standing affects health and longevity*. New York, NY: Henry Holt & Co.

De Waal, F.B. (2005). *Our inner ape*. New York, NY: Riverhead.

Fiske, S.T. (2002). Five core motives: plus or minus five. In S.J. Spencer, S. Fein, M.P., Zanna, & J. Olson (Eds.), *Motivated social perception: The Ontario symposium,* vol.9, pp. 233-246.

Kerr, N.L., & Levine, J.M. (2008). The detection of social exclusion: evolution and beyond. *Group Dynamics: Theory, Research, and Practice,* vol.12, no. 1, pp. 39-52.

Sapolsky, R. (2005), In *"The status syndrome."* Marmot, M. New York, NY: Henry Holt & Co.

Wallerstein, I. (2000). *The essential Wallerstein.* New York, NY: The New Press.

Leary, M.R., & Baumeister, R.F. (2000). The nature and function of self-esteem: Sociometer theory. In M.P. Zanna (Ed.) *Advance in Experimental Social Psychology,* vol.32, pp. 162. San Diego, CA: Academic Press.

Haselton, M.G., & Buss, D.M. (2000). Error management theory: A new perspective on biases in cross-sex mind reading. *Journal of Personality and Social Psychology,* vol. 78, pp. 81-91.

Frank, R.H. (1985). *Choosing the right pond: human behavior and the quest for status.* Oxford, England: Oxford University Press.

Kaus, M. (1995). *The end of equality.* New York, NY: Basic Books.

Easterly, W. (2006). *The white man's burden: Why the West's efforts to aid the rest have done so much ill and so little good.* New York, NY: Penguin Books.

Pinker, S. (2002). *The blank slate: The modern denial of human nature.* New York, NY: Penguin Books.

Obama, B. (2004). Keynote Address, Democratic Convention.

Observations of an Oreo

Gladwell, M. (2005). *Blink: The power of thinking without thinking.* New York, NY: Little Brown & Co.

Goldstein, E.L. (2008). *The price of whiteness: Jews, race, and American identity*. Princeton, NJ: Princeton University Press.

Campbell, D.T. (1958). Common fate, similarity, and other indices of the status of aggregates of person as social entities. *Behavioural Science, 3,* 14–25.

Mayr, E. (2002). The biology of race and the concept of equality. *Daedalus*, vol. 131, no. 1.

Forsyth, D. R. (2010). *Group dynamics* (5th edition). Belmont, CA: Wadsworth.

Hogg, M.A., Sherman, D.K., Diereselhuis, J., Maitner, A,T., & Moffitt, G. (2005) Uncertainty, entitativity, and group identification (2005). *Journal of Experiential Social Psychology.*

Wallerstein, I. (2000). *The essential Wallerstein*. New York, NY: The New Press.

Markus, Hazel R. (2008). Pride, prejudice, and ambivalence: toward a unified theory of race and ethnicity. *American Psychologist,* vol. 63, no. 8.

Kurzban, R., Tooby, J., & Cosmides, L. (2001). Can race be erased? Coalitional computation and social categorization. *PNAS* 98 (28).

Sowell, T. (1998). *Conquest and cultures*. New York, NY: Basic Books.

Flinn, M.V., Geary, D.C., & Ward, C.V. (2005). Ecological dominance, social competition, and coalitional arms races: Why humans evolved extraordinary intelligence. *Evolution and Human Behavior,* 26(1), 10-46.

Fukuyama, F. (1999). *The great disruption: Human nature and the reconstitution of social order*. New York, NY: Simon & Schuster.

Sabini J., & Silver, M. (1983). Dispositional vs. situational interpretations of Milgram's obedience experiments: "The fundamental attributional error". *Journal of the Theory of Social Behaviour*, 13(2), 147-154.

Myers, D.G. (2004). *Exploring psychology*. New York, NY: Macmillan.

Kaus, M. (1995). *The end of equality*. New York, NY: Basic Books

Diamond, J. (1999).*Guns, germs and steel*. New York, NY: W.W. Norton

Milton, G.M. (1964). *Assimilation in American life: The role of race, religion and national origins*. New York, NY: Oxford University Press.

Singer, P. (1981). *The expanding circle: Ethics and sociobiology*. New York, NY: Farrar, Straus & Giroux.

Henderson, M.D. (2009). Psychological distance and group judgments: The effect of physical distance on beliefs about common goals. *Personality and Social Psychology Bulletin*, 35, 1330–1341.

Sowell, T. (1994). *Race and culture: A world view*. New York, NY: Basic Books.

Wilson, E.O. (1999). *Consilience: The unity of knowledge* (Vol. 31). Random House LLC.

Fukuyama, F. (1995). *Trust: The social virtues and the creation of prosperity*. New York, NY: Simon & Schuster.

http://tiny.cc/2u5ytx

Twenge, J.M., Baumeister, R.F., DeWall, C.N., Ciarocco, N.J., & Bartels, J.M. (2007). Social exclusion decreases prosocial behavior. *Journal of Personality and Social Psychology*, 92(1), 56.

Williams, K.D. (2007). Ostracism. *Psychology*, 58(1), 425.

Marmot, M. (2004). *The status syndrome: how social standing affects health and longevity*. New York, NY: Henry Holt & Co.

Hymowitz, K.S. (2005). The Black family: 40 years of lies. *City Journal*, 14.

http://tiny.cc/e75ytx

Pinker, S. (2002) *The blank slate*. New York, NY: Penguin Books

Downey, G., Eccles, J.S., & Chatman, C.M. (2005). *Navigating the future*. Russell Sage Foundation.

Boyd, H. (2007). It's hard out here for a black man! *The Black Scholar*, 29.

Gates Jr., H. L., & West, C. (2011). *The future of the race*. Random House LLC.

Alexander, M. (2012). *The new Jim Crow: Mass incarceration in the age of colorblindness*. The New Press.

http://tiny.cc/cbbdqx

http://tiny.cc/usdxtx Reuniting-Members-of-the-Little-Rock-Nine-Video.

Kurzban, R., Tooby, J., & Cosmides, L. (2001). Can race be erased? Coalitional computation and social categorization. *PNAS* 98 (28).

Apfelbaum, E. (2008). Seeing race and seeming racist? Evaluating strategic colorblindness in social interaction. *Journal of Personality & Social Psychology*, 919 (2008).

http://www.jstor.org/stable/i350389

http://tiny.cc/20bdqx

http://tiny.cc/pw5ytx

Himmelfarb, G. (1999) *One nation, two cultures*. New York, NY: Knopf.

Bloom, A. (2008). *Closing of the American mind*. New York, NY: Simon and Schuster.

The Future of an Albatross

Davis, M. (2001). *Magical urbanism: Latinos reinvent the US city*. Verso.

Galbraith, J.K., & Crook, A. (1958). *The affluent society* (Vol. 534). Boston, MA: Houghton Mifflin.

Hogg, M.A., Sherman, D.K., Dierselhuis, J., Maitner, A.T., & Moffitt, G. (2007). Uncertainty, entitativity, and group identification. *Journal of Experimental Social Psychology*, *43*(1), 135-142.

Hoffer, E. (1951). *The true believer: Thoughts on the nature of mass movements.* (Ed.) New York, NY: Harper and Row.

Baron, R.S., Crawley, K., & Paulina, D. (2003). 13 *Aberrations of power: Leadership in totalist groups. Leadership and power: Identity processes in groups and organizations*, 169.

http://tiny.cc/nx5ytx

Dubos, R.J. (1973). *So human an animal: How we are shaped by surroundings and events.* Transaction Publishers.

www.ingramcontent.com/pod-product-compliance
Lightning Source LLC
Chambersburg PA
CBHW080315290526
45790CB00005B/2048